OPPOSING
VIEWPOINTS®
SERIES

War

Other Books of Related Interest:

Opposing Viewpoints Series

American Values

Civil Liberties

Syria

US Airport Security

At Issue Series

Drones

Piracy on the High Seas

Should the United States Close Its Borders?

Current Controversies Series

Internet Activism

Military Families

Politics and Religion

"Congress shall make
no law . . . abridging
the freedom of speech,
or of the press."

First Amendment to the US Constitution

The basic foundation of our democracy is the First Amendment guarantee of freedom of expression. The Opposing Viewpoints series is dedicated to the concept of this basic freedom and the idea that it is more important to practice it than to enshrine it.

OPPOSING
VIEWPOINTS®
SERIES

I War

David Haugen, Book Editor

GREENHAVEN PRESS
A part of Gale, Cengage Learning

GALE
CENGAGE Learning·

Detroit • New York • San Francisco • New Haven, Conn • Waterville, Maine • London

Elizabeth Des Chenes, *Director, Content Strategy*
Cynthia Sanner, *Publisher*
Douglas Dentino, *Manager, New Product*

For more information, contact:
Greenhaven Press
27500 Drake Rd.
Farmington Hills, MI 48331-3535
Or you can visit our Internet site at gale.cengage.com

For product information and technology assistance, contact us at

Gale Customer Support, 1-800-877-4253
For permission to use material from this text or product, submit all requests online at www.cengage.com/permissions

Further permissions questions can be emailed to permissionrequest@cengage.com

Articles in Greenhaven Press anthologies are often edited for length to meet page requirements. In addition, original titles of these works are changed to clearly present the main thesis and to explicitly indicate the author's opinion. Every effort is made to ensure that Greenhaven Press accurately reflects the original intent of the authors. Every effort has been made to trace the owners of copyrighted material.

Cover Image copyright © Oleg Zabielin/Shutterstock.com.

LIBRARY OF CONGRESS CATALOGING-IN-PUBLICATION DATA

War / David Haugen, book editor.
    pages cm. -- (Opposing viewpoints)
    Includes bibliographical references and index.
    ISBN 978-0-7377-6971-5 (hardcover) -- ISBN 978-0-7377-6972-2 (pbk.)
    1. War (Philosophy) 2. War--Moral and ethical aspects. 3. War--Causes. 4. United States--Military policy. I. Haugen, David M., 1969-
    U21.2.W3589 2013
    355.02--dc23

                                     2013008078

Printed in the United States of America
1 2 3 4 5   17 16 15 14 13

Contents

Chapter 3: How Is America Faring in the War on Terror?

Chapter 4: What Principles Should Guide America's Conduct of War?

Why Consider Opposing Viewpoints?

> *"The only way in which a human being can make some approach to knowing the whole of a subject is by hearing what can be said about it by persons of every variety of opinion and studying all modes in which it can be looked at by every character of mind. No wise man ever acquired his wisdom in any mode but this."*
>
> *John Stuart Mill*

In our media-intensive culture it is not difficult to find differing opinions. Thousands of newspapers and magazines and dozens of radio and television talk shows resound with differing points of view. The difficulty lies in deciding which opinion to agree with and which "experts" seem the most credible. The more inundated we become with differing opinions and claims, the more essential it is to hone critical reading and thinking skills to evaluate these ideas. Opposing Viewpoints books address this problem directly by presenting stimulating debates that can be used to enhance and teach these skills. The varied opinions contained in each book examine many different aspects of a single issue. While examining these conveniently edited opposing views, readers can develop critical thinking skills such as the ability to compare and contrast authors' credibility, facts, argumentation styles, use of persuasive techniques, and other stylistic tools. In short, the Opposing Viewpoints Series is an ideal way to attain the higher-level thinking and reading skills so essential in a culture of diverse and contradictory opinions.

In addition to providing a tool for critical thinking, Opposing Viewpoints books challenge readers to question their own strongly held opinions and assumptions. Most people form their opinions on the basis of upbringing, peer pressure, and personal, cultural, or professional bias. By reading carefully balanced opposing views, readers must directly confront new ideas as well as the opinions of those with whom they disagree. This is not to argue simplistically that everyone who reads opposing views will—or should—change his or her opinion. Instead, the series enhances readers' understanding of their own views by encouraging confrontation with opposing ideas. Careful examination of others' views can lead to the readers' understanding of the logical inconsistencies in their own opinions, perspective on why they hold an opinion, and the consideration of the possibility that their opinion requires further evaluation.

Evaluating Other Opinions

To ensure that this type of examination occurs, Opposing Viewpoints books present all types of opinions. Prominent spokespeople on different sides of each issue as well as well-known professionals from many disciplines challenge the reader. An additional goal of the series is to provide a forum for other, less known, or even unpopular viewpoints. The opinion of an ordinary person who has had to make the decision to cut off life support from a terminally ill relative, for example, may be just as valuable and provide just as much insight as a medical ethicist's professional opinion. The editors have two additional purposes in including these less known views. One, the editors encourage readers to respect others' opinions—even when not enhanced by professional credibility. It is only by reading or listening to and objectively evaluating others' ideas that one can determine whether they are worthy of consideration. Two, the inclusion of such viewpoints encourages the important critical thinking skill of objectively evaluating an author's credentials and bias. This evaluation will illuminate an author's reasons for taking a particular stance on an issue and will aid in readers' evaluation of the author's ideas.

It is our hope that these books will give readers a deeper understanding of the issues debated and an appreciation of the complexity of even seemingly simple issues when good and honest people disagree. This awareness is particularly important in a democratic society such as ours in which people enter into public debate to determine the common good. Those with whom one disagrees should not be regarded as enemies but rather as people whose views deserve careful examination and may shed light on one's own.

Thomas Jefferson once said that "difference of opinion leads to inquiry, and inquiry to truth." Jefferson, a broadly educated man, argued that "if a nation expects to be ignorant and free . . . it expects what never was and never will be." As individuals and as a nation, it is imperative that we consider the opinions of others and examine them with skill and discernment. The Opposing Viewpoints series is intended to help readers achieve this goal.

David L. Bender and Bruno Leone,
Founders

Introduction

> "[The September 11, 2012, attacks on the US diplomatic mission in Benghazi, Libya] were the deliberate work of terrorists who use violence to impose their dark ideology on others . . .; who are fighting to control much of the Middle East today; and who seek to wage perpetual war on the West."
>
> —Massachusetts governor and Republican presidential candidate Mitt Romney, speech at the Virginia Military Institute, October 8, 2012
>
> "[Because of the efforts of US service personnel in Afghanistan, Iraq, and Libya] we can stand here today and say with confidence—the tide of war is receding."
>
> —President Barack Obama, speech commemorating Veterans Day at Arlington National Cemetery, November 11, 2011

The First World War, from 1914–1918, was popularly dubbed "the war to end all wars" because optimistic social critics like British author H.G. Wells—who is one of several commentators credited with begetting the phrase—predicted that the defeat of German militarism in Europe would convince global leaders that the age of imperialism through warfare was at a close. However, as the Great War dragged on and casualties mounted, some pundits deflated the naiveté of such idealistic thinking. Even David Lloyd George, Britain's prime minister during the last two years of the war, supposedly quipped, "This war, like the next war, is a war to end war," implying that every seemingly just global conflict is undertaken with the notion that its conclusion will prove the folly of war. Of course, subsequent civil, international, and multinational conflicts have shown those like Wells to be too rosy in their predictions and those like Lloyd George more accurate even though proving the folly of war has slipped from the purpose of military ventures.

Nearly a century after the end of World War I, wars still occur, drawing in the global community; like the critics and politicians of that time, today's analysts try to provide justifications for beginning conflicts or intervening in them. In the First World War and its global successor, the Allied nations defended their right to go to war in part to protect established borders and curb the ambitions of tyrannical empires. Such justifications persist in more modern wars, but the desires of those who foment war have not been rooted in the grand-scale territorial conquest exhibited by successive German regimes. Indeed, the world has changed; globalization has made borders porous, linking states through economic and communication networks in ways that few could have conceived in 1918. Though international and intra-national wars flare all too regularly, there are perceived threats to the global community as a whole. In the foreword to *Conflict and Cooperation in the Global Commons: A Comprehensive Approach for International Security*, Thomas G. Mahnken, a scholar at the US Naval War College, claims that modern wars are not about protecting borders as much as they are about preserving the global commons, which he defines as not only unowned natural resources and spaces, such as the oceans, but also the free flow of commerce and ideas that exist under international norms agreed upon by free governments. For example, Mahnken argues that the terrorist network al Qaeda poses "nothing short of a brutal attack on the international system" through its rejection of globalization and its defiance of borders. He goes on to indict Iran and North Korea because they have "demonstrated their deep contempt for international norms." In fact, he maintains that the United States and its free-world allies will have to keep up military strength to dissuade or deal with rogue states that might violate international law by seeking out or deploying weapons of mass destruction—which threaten not only human life but also whole environments and patterns of international trade and development. Mahnken believes that just as the world is growing more interconnected, military responses will have to be coordinated to ensure that conflicts do not despoil common resources or disrupt "access" to the global commons or "freedom of action" within them. The justification for war is the commonly held commitment to safeguarding these shared regions and networks.

Former US Air Force officer and counterterrorism expert John Robb agrees with Mahnken that the present threats with potential global impact are those forces that seek to disrupt the processes of globalization. In his book *Brave New War: The Next Stage of Terrorism and the End of Globalization*, Robb points out that global economic, energy, and communication networks are too big for any nation or group of nations to control and keep stable. He insists that today's nonnational guerrilla fighters are "now intentionally introducing instability into these global systems by attacking critical systems, both social and economic." For instance, he describes how, in 2006, al Qaeda operatives tried to detonate cars packed with explosives at the Saudi Arabian oil field at Abqaiq. Though Saudi guards foiled the attack, Robb attests that a successful explosion could have driven the price of oil sky-high and affected energy markets around the globe. He also emphasizes that these irregular armies are using the very channels of globalization to organize attacks on the global system. Thus, small terrorist cells can develop plans and coordinate strategies via cell phone networks, and they can research their targets on the Internet. They can use commercial travel lanes to deposit agents anywhere in the world or even, as the September 11, 2001, commonly known as 9/11, plot against the United States revealed, turn forms of mass travel into weapons of destruction. To Robb, the technological advances employed to bring the world together are ironically the ones terrorists use to rend it apart. He writes, "The threshold necessary for small groups to conduct warfare has finally been breached, and we are only starting to feel its effects."

For Mahnken and Robb, it is not merely that forecasters like H.G. Wells were wrong to suggest that global warfare could ever foster its own end but rather that the notion that international integration would engender a belief in the folly of war. As both Mahnken and Robb argue, the networks of integration are creating the discontent that leads irregular forces to act, and ironically those forces are aided in achieving their goals by the very features of globalization they seek to undo. In the Middle East, oil profits, in part, fund al Qaeda, yet oil networks invite Western investment and dominant business practices. The Internet allows terrorists to connect to each other, yet it also opens the doors to unwanted cultural influences that threaten the ideals for which they stand. And for Mahnken and Robb, it is these non-state actors that will perpetuate conflict in the years to come. As Robb concludes, "Wars between states are now, for all intents and purposes, obsolete. The real remaining threat posed by wars between states, in those rare cases when they do occur by choice, is that they will create a vacuum within which these non-state groups can thrive." Though not dismissive of all the ethnic, environmental, political, and economic reasons that give rise to conflict, he maintains that in the future, it will be irregular armies, not state armies, championing these causes and naming enemies.

Whether Mahnken and Robb are correct in their assessment of twenty-first-century wars, few doubt that the rise of non-state actors has added a new dimension to national and global security. From the pursuit of war in Afghanistan to the religious and economic underpinnings of contemporary conflicts, *Opposing Viewpoints: War* addresses many of the issues foregrounded in any discussion of war in the post-9/11 world. In chapters focused on the questions Can Warfare Be Justified?, What Will Likely Be the Causes of Future Wars?, How Is America Faring in the War on Terror?, and What Principles Should Guide America's Conduct of War?, various experts give their opinions on the appropriateness of warfare as a solution to problems in the new century and the rules of engagement that guide nations such as the United States in pursuing military action as viable national policy. Some, indeed, believe war is rarely a just option in a world built on strengthening international relations and global economies; others warn that strong militaries are needed to ensure the equity of those relationships and to deter those who seek to jeopardize them.

OPPOSING
VIEWPOINTS®
SERIES

CHAPTER 1

Can Warfare Be Justified?

Chapter Preface

The concept of a "just war" has existed in the ruling philosophies of many cultures since ancient times. In Western heritage, the Romans are often cited as early formulators of just war principles. War, to the Romans, was part of the diplomatic relations between states, but it was never to be entered into lightly for it risked incurring the disfavor of the gods. In the Christian era, the fifth-century theologian St. Augustine maintained that God did not disapprove of war as long as it was undertaken to protect peace or dethrone evil. He maintained that it was righteous to defend oneself and others from unprovoked attack and that God-given wisdom would dictate when force was needed. Indeed, Augustine coined the phrase when he wrote in his treatise *The City of God*, "the wise man will wage just wars." St. Thomas Aquinas, a Catholic scholar, resurrected Augustine's notions in the thirteenth century and described the conditions under which war could be justified. He asserted that a war must not be waged for gain or power, though it must be enacted by a governing body that has the power and authority to make such fateful decisions. Aquinas also insisted that all just wars should have peace as their motive and aim.

In the seventeenth century, amidst ongoing warfare between Catholic and Protestant nations in Europe, Dutch jurist Hugo Grotius drafted *On the Law of War and Peace*, a work that combined Christian just war scholarship and natural law to codify what he understood to be the legitimate reasons any rational state might have to engage in conflict. Grotius separated the justifications for going to war (*jus ad bellum*) from the just conduct of war (*jus in bello*) and, as part of his larger endeavor to formulate binding international laws, he fashioned a list of martial rules that still influence just war theory and international policy today. According to Grotius, a nation was justified in going to war if the threat to the state was immediate, if the force used was proportionate to threat, and if that force was adequate to defend the nation. No longer was there an assertion that war was backed by divine providence; rather just war involved a balancing of imminent threat and adequate force in the secular relations between states.

As the viewpoints in the following chapter illustrate, just war theory is still currently discussed in national and international policy arenas. The US wars in Afghanistan and Iraq are but two recent incidences that have brought out philosophers and pundits to address both America's justifications for war and its military conduct in the field. Some defend America's motives under the Grotian doctrine of "immediate threat" while others question whether the country's motives were tainted by a desire for greed and power. Such debate, however, has made some people skeptical of the value of laws pertaining to just warfare. That is, if governments can bend the theory to justify their actions, then accountability fails. In a speech to the United States Military Academy at West Point on April 20, 2006, social critic and philosopher Noam Chomsky claimed that powerful nations such as the United States typically consider themselves above the laws that would restrict unilateral actions believed to be in their best interests. Still, Chomsky contends that "the codification of laws of war has over time had a notable civilizing effect," yet he goes on to state, "but the gap between professed ideals and actual practice is much too large to be tolerated."

| *"No decision is more fateful than the decision of a government to employ military force."*

War Can Be Justified When It Is the Best Policy Option

Richard N. Haass

Richard N. Haass is the president of the Council on Foreign Relations, a nonprofit American think tank focused on foreign policy issues. From January 2001 to June 2003, Haass served as director of policy planning for the US Department of State. In the following viewpoint, Haass argues that traditional "just war" theory is inadequate because it is too subjective and restrictive, potentially sacrificing lives while policy makers debate what constitutes a just cause and what authority has the power to sanction military action. Instead, Haass contends that wars must simply be justifiable, meaning that the government has either exhausted its alternative methods of conflict resolution or that swift action has considerable domestic and international support. In such cases, Haass believes even wars of choice can be justified if they are the best policy option to resolve a crisis with the least cost to humanity.

As you read, consider the following questions:

1. As Haass reiterates, what three conditions did St. Thomas Aquinas insist were necessary to justify war?

2. Does Haass believe the Vietnam War was a war of choice or a war of necessity?

3. Why does the author consider the second Iraq war to be an unjustifiable war?

Should the United States attack Iran if we learn it has begun to enrich uranium to the level required for a nuclear bomb? What about attacking North Korea if it appears too close to producing a nuclear warhead small enough to place inside a missile? Or sending troops into Pakistan if the government loses what little control it has over its western regions and terrorists take hold?

No decision is more fateful than the decision of a government to employ military force. Except in the most clear-cut cases, such decisions are also difficult. As a result, just war theory has for centuries provided useful guidance to policy makers, clergy, citizens, and soldiers alike. But just war theory is too subjective and confining for today's real-world threats.

Finding Justification

A more useful concept is that of justifiable war.

Just war theory today is a composite that has evolved from ideas developed by various religious figures. In the 5th century, St. Augustine discussed in *The City of God* the circumstances under which killing could be justified and empires legitimately expanded. In the 13th century, St. Thomas Aquinas laid out a more elaborate just war doctrine in his *Summa Theologica*. He wrote that three conditions were necessary to make a war just: it must be ordered by a competent authority; the cause must be just; and the combatants must have "a right intention, so that they intend the advancement of good, or the avoidance of evil."

Modern just war guidance involves both the decision to go to war (*jus ad bellum*) and how to fight one (*jus in bello*). This latter set of criteria focuses on proportionality (how much force is used), targeting (avoiding noncombatants), and means (avoiding certain classes of weapons).

Most of the debate, however, reflects the more basic decision of when to go to war. Building on the writings of both Augustine and Aquinas, there must be a just cause as well as a decision by a competent authority sanctioning the undertaking. War must be a last resort. There must be a good chance of success. And projected benefits must outweigh projected costs. The theory also holds that all the criteria need to be present before a war can be deemed just and hence undertaken.

Problem with Just War Theory

One problem with just war theory is that it is too subjective. What constitutes a just cause is in the eyes of the beholder, as are the probability of success and any estimate of likely costs and benefits.

Just war theory is also too confining. Is the United Nations Security Council the only competent authority, or was NATO's [North Atlantic Treaty Organization's] approval enough to make the Kosovo war [an armed conflict that lasted from February 1998 to June 1999] just? Waging war only as a last resort means risking the lives of many while other policies are tried and found wanting.

That's why justifiable war is a more useful concept. Justifiable wars undoubtedly include wars of necessity, that is, wars in which the most vital interests of a country are threatened and where there are no promising alternatives to using force. World War Two and the first Iraq war of 1990–1991 following [Iraqi dictator] Saddam Hussein's invasion of Kuwait would qualify, as would wars of self-defense.

Hypothesizing Iraqi Attitudes to the Justness of a US-Led Invasion of Iraq

Imagine, for example, that you and your children are living under a ruthless regime similar to that of pre-war Iraq. You live in constant fear that you will be arrested and tortured, either for speaking out against the government or simply because someone reports you to the authorities. In the past, tens of thousands of your people have been killed in ruthless campaigns of oppression, and you do not know if or when another such campaign may be mounted. Finally, you fear for the future of your children. Not only will they likely experience the same oppression and systematic terror you face (including the risk of being forced to serve in the military or oppressive apparatus of the state), they will also be subject to the harm of being indoctrinated by state propaganda.

If, under this scenario, a foreign power were considering an invasion to overthrow the current regime, with the promise to help the people institute more democratic institutions and a just rule of law, I suspect most people would agree that this opportunity would be worth the risks of war—even though those risks include death, horrible maiming and other severe hardships, and even if, as was surely true among Iraqis, there is some doubt about the intentions of the foreign powers.

David Mellow,
"Iraq: A Morally Justified Resort to War,"
Journal of Applied Philosophy, *August 2006.*

Justifying Wars of Choice

The question is whether wars of choice can also be justifiable. By definition, wars of choice tend to involve less than vital interests and the existence of alternative policies. Vietnam,

Kosovo and Bosnia were all wars of choice. So, too, was the second Iraq war begun in 2003.

Are wars of choice ever justifiable? The answer is "yes" when using force is the best available policy option. The argument that the goal is worthy and that war is the best option for pursuing it should be strong enough to garner considerable domestic and international support. More important, the case should be persuasive that using military force will accomplish more good for more people at a lower cost than diplomacy, sanctions, or inaction.

By this standard, the second Iraq war was not justifiable, as the United States could have done more to contain Saddam through strengthening sanctions. There was a decided lack of international support. And even before the war, it was argued and could have been known that the likely costs would be great and the accomplishments modest.

But what about the future? The concept of justifiable war is not simply one for history. Iran, North Korea, Pakistan, Afghanistan—all are potential theaters for new or intensified U.S. military action. The question is not whether they would constitute just wars. That is too impractical a standard. The question in the real world is whether they would be justifiable—to Congress, to the American people, to the world. It is a question President [Barack] Obama will have to answer.

> *"The reasons given to justify a war's being fought . . . generally amount to claims that cannot support a strong case."*

War Can Rarely Be Justified

Robert Higgs

In the following viewpoint, Robert Higgs argues that traditional justifications for sending a country to war are usually flawed. In his view, war is almost never a necessity, nor is it the only way of halting the actions of tyrannical or rogue leaders. Higgs also dismantles the common claim that war is simply a facet of human relations and will always exist. He encourages citizens to interrogate the justifications governments give for going to war and force these officials to demonstrate the necessity of sacrificing lives for the cause. By doing so, he insists, the justifications will typically crumble, and the rationality of peace will prevail. Robert Higgs is a senior fellow in political economy for the Independent Institute—a nonprofit economic and social issue research organization—and the editor of the institute's quarterly journal, the Independent Review.

Robert Higgs, "War Is Horrible, but . . . ," *Independent Review*, vol. 17, no. 2, Fall 2012, pp. 305–316.

As you read, consider the following questions:

1. What are some of the methods of "shunning" that Higgs believes could be useful diplomatic and coercive tools to stop evil conduct on the part of tyrannical governments?

2. Why does Higgs claim that invoking biblical authority "doesn't get us very far" in justifying warfare?

3. How does Higgs refute the argument that continually preparing for war will help preserve peace?

Anyone who has done even a little reading about the theory and practice of war—whether in political theory, international relations, theology, history, or common journalistic commentary—has encountered a sentence of the form "War is horrible, but. . . ." In this construction, the phrase that follows the conjunction explains why a certain war was (or now is or someday will be) an action that ought to have been (or still ought to be) undertaken, notwithstanding its admitted horrors. The frequent, virtually formulaic use of this expression attests that nobody cares to argue, say, that war is a beautiful, humane, uplifting, or altogether splendid course of action and therefore the more often people fight, the better.

Apologies for War

Some time ago—in the late nineteenth and early twentieth centuries, for example—one might have encountered a writer such as Theodore Roosevelt who forthrightly affirmed that war is manly and invigorating for the nation and the soldiers who engage in it: War keeps a nation from "getting soft." Although this opinion is no longer expressed openly with great frequency, something akin to it may yet survive, as [journalist and war correspondent] Chris Hedges has argued in *War Is a Force That Gives Us Meaning* (2002). Nowadays, however, even those who find meaning for their lives by involvement in war, perhaps even only marginal or symbolic involvement, do not often extol war as such.

They are likely instead to justify a nation's engagement in war by calling attention to alternative and even more horrible outcomes that, retrospectively, would have occurred if the nation had not gone to war or, prospectively, will occur if it does not go to war. This seemingly reasonable "balancing" form of argument often sounds stronger than it really is, especially when it is made more or less in passing. People may easily be swayed by a weak argument, however, if they fail to appreciate the defects of the typically expressed "horrible, but" apology for war.

Rather than plow through various sources on my bookshelves to compile examples, I have availed myself of modern technology. A Google search for the exact phrase "war is horrible but" on May 21, 2012, identified 58,100 instances of it. Rest assured that this number is smaller than the entire universe of such usage—some instances most likely have yet to be captured electronically. Among the examples I drew from the World Wide Web are the following fourteen statements. I identify the person who made the statement only when he is well known.

Refuting the Necessity of War

"War is horrible. But no one wants to see a world in which a regime with no regard whatsoever for international law—for the welfare of its own people—or for the will of the United Nations—has weapons of mass destruction." (U.S. deputy secretary of state Richard Armitage [2003])

This statement was part of a speech Richard Armitage gave on January 21, 2003, shortly before the U.S. government unleashed its armed forces to inflict "shock and awe" on the nearly defenseless people of Iraq. The speech repeated the [George W.] Bush administration's standard prewar litany of accusations, including several claims later revealed to be false, so it cannot be viewed as anything but bellicose propaganda. Yet it does not differ much from what many others were saying at the time.

On its own terms, the statement scarcely serves to justify a war. The conditions outlined—a regime's disregard of international law, its own people's well-being, and the will of the United Nations, combined with possession of weapons of mass destruction—apply to several nations. They no more justified a military attack on Iraq than they justified an attack on Pakistan, France, India, Russia, China, the United Kingdom, Israel, or the United States itself.

"War is terrible, war is horrible, but war is also at times necessary and the only means of stopping evil."

The *only* means of stopping evil? How can such singularity exist? Has evil conduct never been stopped except by war? For example, has shunning—exclusion from commerce, financial systems, communications, transportation systems, and other means of international cooperation—never served to discipline an evil nation-state? Might it do so if seriously tried? (If these questions give the impression that I am suggesting the possibility of resorting to embargo or blockade, that perception is not exactly correct. Although I support various forms of voluntary, peaceful withdrawal of cooperation with evildoing states, I do not endorse state-enforced—that is, violent or potentially violent—embargoes and blockades.) Why must we leap to the conclusion that only war will serve, when other measures have scarcely even been considered, much less seriously attempted? If war is really as horrible as everyone says, it would seem that we have a moral obligation to try very hard to achieve the desired suppression of evil doing by means other than resorting to warfare, which is itself always a manifest evil, even when it is seemingly the lesser one. . . .

"You may think that the Iraq war is horrible, but there may be some times when you can justify [going to war]."

Perhaps war *can* be justified at "some times," but this statement itself in no way shows that the Iraq war can be justified, and it seems all too obvious that it cannot be. If it could have been justified, the government that launched it would not have had to resort to a succession of weak excuses for waging it, each such excuse being manifestly inadequate or simply false. The obvious insufficiency of any of the reasons put forward explains why so many of us put so much time and effort into trying to divine exactly what *did* impel the Bush administration's rush to war. . . .

War Need Not Always Exist in Human Affairs

"Of course war is horrible, but it will always exist, and I'm sick of these pacifist [expletive deleted] ruining any shred of political decency that they can manage."

Many people have observed that wars have recurred for thousands of years and therefore will probably continue to occur from time to time. The unstated insinuation seems to be that in view of war's long-running recurrence, nothing can be done about it, so we should all grow up and admit that war is as natural and hence as unalterable as the sun's rising in the east each morning. Warfare is an inescapable aspect of "how the world works."

This outlook contains at least two difficulties. First, many other conditions also have had long-running histories: for example, reliance on astrologers as experts in foretelling the future; affliction with cancers; submission to rulers who claim to dominate their subjects by virtue of divine descent or appointment; and many others. People eventually overcame or continue to work to overcome each of these long-established conditions. Science revealed that astrology is nothing more than an elaborate body of superstition; scientists and doctors have discovered how to control or cure certain forms of cancer and are attempting to do the same for other forms; and citizens learned to laugh at the pretensions of rulers who claim divine descent or appointment (at least, they *had* learned to do so until George W. Bush successfully revived this doctrine among the benighted rubes who form the Republican base). Because wars spring in large part from people's stupidity, ignorance, and gullibility, it is conceivable that alleviation of these conditions might have the effect of diminishing the frequency of warfare, if not of eliminating it altogether.

Second, even if nothing *can* be done to stop the periodic outbreak of war, it does not follow that we ought to shut up and accept every war without complaint. No serious person expects, say, that evil can be eliminated from the human condition, yet we condemn it and struggle against its realization in human affairs. We strive to divert potential evildoers from their malevolent course of action. Scientists and doctors continue to seek cures for cancers that have afflicted humanity for millennia. Even conditions that cannot be wholly eliminated can sometimes be mitigated, but only if someone tries to mitigate them. War should belong to this class of events.

Finally, whatever else might be said about the pacifists, one may surely assert that if everyone were a pacifist, no wars would occur. Pacifism may be criticized on various grounds, as it always has been and still is, but to say that pacifists "lack any shred of political decency" seems itself to be an indecent description. Remember: War is horrible, as everybody now concedes but many immediately put out of mind. . . .

The Pretext of Saving Innocent Lives

"[Certain writers] all agreed that war is horrible but said the Bible gives government the authority to wage war to save innocent lives."

For almost two thousand years, biblical scholars have been disputing what Christians may and may not do in regard to war. The dispute continues today, so the matter is certainly not resolved among devout Christians. Even if Christians may

The Danger of Normalizing War by Seeking to Justify It

At stake in the effort to justify war is not simply some academic exercise. At stake in the effort to legalize and justify war is the demand to normalize war. On the one hand, this is impossible. War, like any deeply human activity, will exceed all efforts by humans to control and to regulate it. On the other hand, however, the desire to normalize war is also misplaced. What is needed, rather, is a determination to recall that justice, and not merely justification, has a place in war. Instead of the justifications offered by just war theorizing, we must demand that those who fight and we who think about war not blind ourselves to the illumination of justice amidst the fog of war's justifications.

Roger Berkowitz, "Should We Justify War?," in
Just War in Religion and Politics. Eds. Jacob Neusner,
Bruce D. Chilton, and R.E. Tully. Lanham, MD:
University Press of America, 2013.

go to war to save innocent lives, however, a big question remains: Is the government going to war for this purpose or for one of the countless other purposes that lead governments to make war? Saving the innocent makes an appealing excuse, but it is often, if not always, only a pretext. "Just war" writers from [fifth-century philosopher and theologian St.] Augustine to [thirteenth-century theologian and scholar St.] Thomas Aquinas to [seventeenth-century legal philosopher Hugo] Grotius to the latest contributors have agonized over the ready availability of such pretexts and warned against the wickedness of advancing them when the real motives are less justifiable or even plainly immoral.

For centuries, European combatants on all sides invoked God's blessing for their wars against one another. As recently as World War II, the Germans claimed to have "Gott mit Uns," a declaration that adorned the belt buckles of Wehrmacht soldiers in *both* world wars. Strange to say, in 1917 and 1918 Christian ministers of the gospel in pulpits across the United States were assuring their congregations that *their* nation-state was engaged in a "war for righteousness" (the title of Richard M. Gamble's [2003] splendid book about this repellent episode). So the invocation of biblical authority really doesn't get us very far: The enemy may be invoking the same authority.

Nowadays, of course, one side invokes the Jewish and Christian God, whereas the other calls on the blessing of Allah. Whether this bifurcated manner of gaining divine sanction for the commission of mass murder and mayhem among the sons of Abraham represents progress or not, I leave to the learned theologians. . . .

The Ludicrous Argument of Maintaining Peace Through War

"Of course, war is horrible, but at present it's still the only guarantee to maintain peace."

This statement as it stands is self-contradictory because it affirms that the only way to make sure that we will have peace is by going to war. Perhaps, if we are feeling generous, we may interpret the statement as the time-honored exhortation that to maintain the peace, we should *prepare* for war, hoping that by dissuading aggressors from moving against us, our preparation will preserve the peace. Although this reworded policy is not self-contradictory, it is dangerous because the preparation we make for war may itself move us toward actually going to war. For example, preparation for war may entail increasing the number of military officers and allowing the top brass to exert greater influence in making foreign policy. Those officers may believe that without war their careers will go nowhere, and so they may tilt their advice to civilian authorities toward risking or actually making war even when peace might easily be preserved. Likewise, military suppliers may use their political influence to foster international suspicions and fears that otherwise might be allayed. Wars are not good for business in general, but they are good for the munitions contractors. Certain legislators may develop an interest in militarism; perhaps it helps them to attract campaign contributions from arms contractors, veterans' groups, and members of the National Guard and military reserve organizations. Pretty soon we may find ourselves dealing, as President Dwight D. Eisenhower did, with a military-industrial-congressional complex, and we may find that it packs a great deal of political punch and acts in a way that, all things considered, diminishes the chance of keeping the country at peace.

The Burden of Proof Is on the Warmongers

From the foregoing commentary, a recurrent theme may be extracted: Those who argue that "war is horrible, but . . ." nearly always use this rhetorical construction not to frame a genuinely serious and honest balancing of reasons for and against war, but only to acknowledge what cannot be hidden—that war is horrible—and then to pass on immediately to an affirmation that notwithstanding the horrors, whose actual forms and dimensions they neither specify nor examine in detail, a certain war ought to be fought.

The reasons given to justify a war's being fought, however, generally amount to claims that cannot support a strong case. They often are not even bona fide reasons, but mere propaganda, especially when they emanate from official sources. They sometimes rest on historical errors, such as the claim that the armed forces in past wars have somehow kept foreigners from depriving us of our liberties. And the case for war usually rests on ill-founded speculation about what will happen if we do not go to war.

People need to recognize, however, that government officials and their running dogs in the media, among others, are not soothsayers. None of us knows the future, but these interested parties lack a disinterested motive for making a careful, well-informed forecast. . . .

The government generally relies on marshaling patriotic emotion and reflexive loyalty rather than on making a sensible case for going to war. Much of the discussion that does take place is a sham because the government officials who pretend to listen to other opinions, as U.S. leaders did most recently during 2002 and early 2003, have already decided what they are going to do, no matter what other people may say. The rulers know that once the war starts, nearly everybody will fall into line and "support the troops."

If someone demands that the skeptic about war offer constructive criticism, here is my proposal: Always insist that the *burden of proof* rests heavily on the warmonger. This protocol, which is now anything but standard operating procedure, is eminently judicious precisely because, as we all recognize, war is horrible. Given its horrors, which in reality are much greater than most people appreciate, it only makes sense that those who propose to enter into those horrors make a very, very strong case for doing so. If they cannot—and I submit that they almost never can—then people will serve their interests best by declining an invitation to war. As a rule, the most rational, humane, and auspicious course of action is indeed to give peace a chance.

"Some threats to international peace and security are so potentially damaging that preventing them in advance may be preferable to remedying their effects."

Preventive War Can Be Justified by Adhering to Strict International Legal Standards

Abraham D. Sofaer

In the following viewpoint, Abraham D. Sofaer claims that countries have routinely violated United Nations (UN) protocols defining the legality of undertaking preventive military action in defending their national security or intervening against human rights abuses in other lands. Sofaer maintains that many of these preventive actions—though illegal by UN standards—were justified by having widespread international support and clearly defined objectives. Sofaer contends that the United Nations should adopt new standards that would sanction preventive wars in which the cost of inaction would be more detrimental than the use of force. He believes that by adhering to specific tests that would prove the action was legitimate (namely, showing the urgency of the threat and that other nonviolent options had failed),

Abraham D. Sofaer, "The Best Defense?," *Foreign Affairs*, v. 89, no. 1, January/February 2010, pp. 109–118. Reprinted by permission of FOREIGN AFFAIRS. Copyright 2010 by the Council on Foreign Relations Inc. www.ForeignAffairs.com.

a nation using preventive force could avoid international criticism and justify its deed. Abraham D. Sofaer was a US State Department legal advisor from 1985–1990. In 1994 he obtained his current position as a senior fellow in foreign policy and national security affairs at the Hoover Institution, a US public policy think tank at Stanford University.

As you read, consider the following questions:

1. What is the difference between preventive war and preemptive war, according to Sofaer?

2. How does Sofaer use the Israeli bombing of the Osirak nuclear reactor in Iraq to exemplify his claim that international opinion of a preventive military strike can change over time?

3. As the author relates, what did the 2004 report of the High-Level Panel on Threats, Challenges and Change recommend that the UN Security Council adopt?

After 9/11 [referring to the September 11, 2001, terrorist attacks on the United States], U.S. President George W. Bush announced his determination to do whatever was necessary to prevent future terrorist attacks against the United States. Following the lead of several countries that had recently come to similar conclusions after their own bitter experiences including India, Israel, Japan, Russia, Spain, and the United Kingdom—the United States tightened its immigration laws; increased the protection of its borders, ports, and infrastructure; criminalized providing "material support" for terrorist groups; and tore down the wall between the intelligence agencies and law enforcement agencies, which had crippled counterterrorist efforts for decades. Washington did not authorize preventive detention, as other countries had, but it used other measures to hold persons against whom criminal charges could not be brought—thereby preventing terrorist attacks. The U.S. government also led or joined various international efforts aimed at warding off new dangers, such as the Proliferation Security Initiative, through which over 70 states cooperate to interdict the movement of nuclear materials across international borders.

But the Bush administration's call for preventive action went further: It endorsed using force against states that supported terrorism or failed to prevent it. This was a particularly controversial position, since using (or threatening to use) preventive force across international borders is generally considered to be a violation of international law: The International Court of Justice (ICJ) and most international legal authorities currently construe the United Nations (UN) charter as prohibiting any use of force not sanctioned by the UN Security Council, with the exception of actions taken in self-defense against an actual or imminent state-sponsored "armed attack."

Now that the Bush administration is no longer in power, some argue that its approach to this subject should be shelved. But the objective of preventing terrorist threats before they are realized—rather than primarily treating terrorism as a crime warranting punishment after the fact—is now established as an essential element of U.S. national security. Indeed, in 2008, Barack Obama, then a presidential candidate, told the American Society of International Law that "the preventive use of force may be necessary, but rarely." And Vice President Joe Biden announced in February 2009, "We'll strive to act preventively, not preemptively, to avoid whenever possible the choice of last resort between the risks of war and the dangers of inaction." Other senior officials have made similar statements, both before joining the Obama administration and since.

Modern Threats to National Security

The case for considering preventive force stems largely from the threat posed by terrorists, especially their potential use of weapons of mass destruction (WMD). But it is justified by other threats as well, including the proliferation of WMD to irresponsible or fanatical regimes; the spread of criminal activities, such as piracy and drug and human trafficking; and genocide or other massive violations of human rights.

The UN, NATO [North Atlantic Treaty Organization], other regional organizations, and many individual countries agree that these threats exist and need to be countered. The UN High-Level Panel on Threats, Challenges and Change, appointed by Secretary-General Kofi Annan, concluded in December 2004 that "in the world of the twenty-first century, the international community does have to be concerned about nightmare scenarios combining terrorists, weapons of mass destruction and irresponsible states, and much more besides, which may conceivably justify the use of force, not just reactively but preventively and before a latent threat becomes imminent."

Preventive action seeks to counter threats before they are imminent. It is thus distinguished from preemptive action, which, in [early nineteenth-century politician and three-time secretary of state] Daniel Webster's classic formulation, is taken when a government has "a necessity of self-defence, instant, overwhelming, leaving no choice of means, and no moment for deliberation." In contrast, preventive action seeks to head off dangers that are further in the future and therefore less tangible, less likely to occur, and possibly more avoidable through diplomacy. Prevention is not considered an act of self-defense under the UN charter. But although these distinctions are valid and significant, they can be overstated.

Many contemporary threats do not involve conventional forces that can be observed as they prepare to attack; rather, they involve unconventional uses of force that remain invisible until their sudden deployment. Such unconventional uses of force can seldom be preempted at their moment of imminence. Moreover, many contemporary threats do not qualify as "armed attacks" under current international law, since they come from non-state actors, are aimed at a state's citizens or interests outside of its territory, or are considered insufficiently substantial to entitle a state to resort to the full range of actions allowed in cases of recognized self-defense. Some threats stem from criminal activities, not "armed attacks," and some involve governments targeting their own populations via massive deprivations of human rights. All these unconventional threats can be very serious and may result in great potential harm. Although international uses of force to counter such threats would be considered illegal without Security Council approval, such actions could be as vital to maintaining international peace and security as the actions of domestic law enforcement are to maintaining domestic security. . . .

International Response to Preventive Action

Despite the illegality and the risks involved, states have used unauthorized force for preventive purposes in well over 100 instances since the UN charter was signed in 1945. This has happened in part because during the Cold War [a period of tension between the United States and the Soviet Union during the second half of the twentieth century] stalemate, the Security Council failed to perform its duty to maintain international peace and security. Instead of cooperating on the council, the two superpowers competed to support proxies, which, in turn, sought power and territory across the world. In some cases, parties used unauthorized force to overthrow colonial regimes. These coups (which had no preventive purpose) demonstrated the unwillingness of states to be bound by narrow legal limits on the use of force, including the requirement of Security Council authorization. Other unauthorized uses of force were preventive, including hostage-rescue operations, abductions of criminals and terrorists, targeted killings, attacks on terrorists and their infrastructure, actions to prevent the subversion of established governments, the dis-

ruption of WMD development, actions to prevent gross violations of human rights, preventive cyber attacks, and preventive war.

Although virtually all these were technically illegal, they
elicited different reactions from the international community
depending on their purpose, duration, and consequences.
Some unauthorized actions have been condemned, many have
been accepted without comment, and some have even been
widely praised or formally supported. . . .

Although interventions have often earned criticism when
they have seemed to advance national interests rather than
objectives based on the UN charter, the motive has often mat-
tered less than the result. Consider two events from the 1970s.
In late 1978, Vietnam invaded Cambodia to remove the
Khmer Rouge from power and to limit China's control in
Southeast Asia. And in 1979, the Tanzanian army deposed Idi
Amin in Uganda in order to prevent him from attempting to
capture part of Tanzania. Ultimately, Vietnam was criticized
more for occupying Cambodia too long than for having over-
thrown the murderous Pol Pot regime. And although Amin
rightly complained that he was attacked before any of his
forces had even entered Tanzania, the UN Security Council
and then UN Secretary-General Kurt Waldheim simply ignored his complaints, no doubt recognizing the benefits of his
removal from power.

Likewise, international responses to unauthorized interventions (preventive and otherwise) have depended on the
credibility of the intervening states' justifications. For example,
Israel's 1976 operation to rescue Israeli and Jewish passengers
from a hijacked plane at Uganda's Entebbe [International]
Airport was deemed acceptable, since Amin had embraced the
cause of the kidnappers and the involvement of Israel was tai-
lored to the narrow objective it had claimed. The United
States' 1983 invasion of Grenada, on the other hand which
was also a hostage-rescue operation, in that over 500 U.S.

medical students were being barred from leaving the island, was widely opposed because in addition to rescuing the students, the United States used the opportunity to oust the country's new leaders and to eliminate all Cuban political influence.

International attitudes toward some categories of actions have changed over time, which further complicates the task of evaluating the acceptability of these actions. For example, the UN Security Council at first condemned Israel's 1981 bombing of Iraq's Osirak nuclear reactor. But a decade later, after Iraq repeatedly attacked other countries and used chemical weapons at home and abroad, Israel's strike received widespread praise. And in 2007, by which time the world had grown increasingly concerned about the proliferation of WMD, Israel's attack on what seemed to be the foundations of a nuclear reactor in Syria was barely criticized.

The use of force to prevent humanitarian disasters (or halt their escalation) also elicits more support today than it would have when the UN charter was adopted. The movement to establish a "responsibility to protect" reflects a growing acceptance of the need to prevent gross violations of human rights, even those taking place within another country's borders. The 1999 U.S.-led intervention in Kosovo was technically illegal because the UN Security Council did not approve it, but it was sanctioned by NATO and widely supported. . . .

Establishing an International Standard on Preventive War

The existence of a UN Security Council with the will and the means to prevent threats to international peace and security would help reduce the need for unauthorized preventive action. But although the council has sometimes undertaken specific peacekeeping operations; responded to aggression; and adopted important rules regarding terrorism, the proliferation

The Difficult Justification of Preventive War

While preventive war is not unjust, it is extremely difficult to justify. The [US] National Security Strategy clearly states the manner in which we will determine those threats that require preemptive or preventive strike. When making the argument on anticipatory self-defense it is important to consider the criteria of both sufficient and imminent threat, for this has long been a standard by which the war convention has judged the legitimacy of a first strike. International law recognizes that preemptive strikes, as a matter of self-defense, can be performed against threats somewhat short of imminent, yet significant enough to cause just fear. The principles of proportionality and last resort must also be applied if prevention is to be viewed as just. Failure to consider all reasonable options, to include the use of force, weakens the moral position of the user and implies that violence is the preferred method of conflict resolution.

Donald K. Ulrich, "A Moral Argument on Preventive War," US Army War College Strategy Research Project, March 18, 2005.

of WMD, and human rights, it has often failed to enforce its own resolutions to prevent threats from being realized.

One way to remedy such inadequacies is to make sure that the existing rules serve the UN charter's purposes. Some aspects of the law governing the use of force—including the concepts of necessity and proportionality—remain universally accepted. But other aspects are seldom taken seriously and deserve review and amendment. For example, states could read article 2, paragraph 4, of the charter more literally—as prohibiting the threat or use of force when it is employed to undermine the territorial integrity of states "or in any other manner inconsistent with the purposes of the United Nations." They could also recognize an exception to article 2, paragraph 4, permitting compelling humanitarian interventions or the use of force for objectives approved as proper by the Security Council. Also, the right of self-defense under article 51 could more often be treated as "inherent" (as is written in the article) and thereby consistent with the historic right to use force for that purpose. And, as suggested by the British Foreign Office, states could understand the meaning of "imminent" to include situations in which a known terrorist group had both the intent to carry out attacks and the ability to do so without being detected. This would expand the concept's meaning to fit a world in which grave threats can be realized at a time and a place impossible to anticipate in advance.

Instead of accepting such changes, which increasingly reflect actual state practice, the ICJ has continued to support and craft rules that effectively protect terrorists, proliferators, and irresponsible states. In 1986, for example, the ICJ rejected El Salvador's claim to self-defense against Nicaragua, which was aiding rebels seeking to undermine the elected Salvadoran government. By doing so, the ICJ effectively denied El Salvador the right to cooperate with the United States in an exercise of collective self-defense. In 2004, the ICJ found that Israel's right of self-defense did not apply to protecting itself against attacks on its population (including suicide bombings) by non-state actors. This meant that Israel could not legally build a fence or take other self-defense measures on any territory beyond its internationally accepted borders. Similarly, the next year, the court ruled that Uganda had no right to self-defense against rebels attacking it from the Democratic Republic of the Congo because the attackers had not been sent by the Congolese government, even though that government had failed to stop them, as international law requires. These decisions—along with the ICJ's refusal to treat as precedents those uses of force that the international community has widely accepted as just, such as NATO's intervention in Kosovo—have undermined, rather than enhanced, the objectives of the UN charter.

One possible reaction to international law's failure to deal effectively with current threats would be to treat it as irrelevant and regard national self-interest as the only reliable guide for when to use force, preventive or otherwise. But the United States cannot and should not respond this way. It is obliged to abide by the UN charter's rules, and it has a strong interest in having other states do so as well. Disregarding international law would free all states to act as they please when the goal should be to encourage them to act in ways that advance universally accepted objectives.

Separating Legitimacy from Legality

The 2004 report of the secretary-general's High-Level Panel on Threats, Challenges and Change suggested a far better approach to enhancing international security. The panel was unwilling to abandon existing international legal norms, but— recognizing both that the UN Security Council does not always act when it should and that the legality of a use of force does not assure its wisdom or utility—it proposed that the Security Council adopt "a set of agreed guidelines, going directly not to whether force can legally be used but whether, as a matter of good conscience and good sense, it should be." The panel, in other words, rightly acknowledged that the legitimacy of an action can differ from its legality.

Legality is relevant in determining an action's legitimacy, but so are other values and norms, including the propriety of dealing effectively with substantial threats to charter-based values. The UN Security Council's decision to deny weapons to victims of ethnic and religious abuse in Yugoslavia in the early 1990s, for example, was legal but arguably illegitimate, whereas NATO's unauthorized use of force to prevent abuses in Kosovo was illegal but arguably legitimate.

Using legitimacy as a guide in determining whether to use preventive force would allow states to take into account a broader range of considerations than current international law typically dictates. Such states would weigh not only their own views regarding possible uses of preventive force but also the views of other states, nongovernmental organizations, and knowledgeable or interested groups and individuals (including UN agencies, regional organizations, religious leaders, and others). Legitimacy is not a yes-or-no proposition but a matter of degree; it does not demand the definitive conclusions required of legal opinions.

The concept of legitimacy, moreover, can be made more concrete through the establishment of a process to judge state conduct according to various important standards, such as the seriousness of a perceived threat, the necessity of using force to counter the threat, the proportionality of the force used, the extent of international support for the action in question, the action's consistency with the values of the UN charter, the strength of the evidence supporting the intervention, and whether the action meets the chief criterion of "just war," that is, whether its expected benefits outweigh its potential costs.

In addition to subjecting potential preventive actions to these standards, states should take procedural steps to help establish the actions' legitimacy. Although preventive actions must sometimes be secret in order to be effective, their causes are often well known and should be discussed within the UN Security Council in advance. In all instances, a state that has taken preventive action should report the action to the council after the fact in order to justify its conduct. And states that use force preventively should accept accountability for errors; they should conduct thorough inquiries of their actions and seriously consider paying compensation to the victims of their mistakes.

The Value of Legitimacy Tests

Some threats to international peace and security are so potentially damaging that preventing them in advance may be preferable to remedying their effects. Prevention can often be achieved by means short of force (including diplomacy, sanctions, and deterrence), and the unauthorized preventive use of force should be considered only as a last resort, when all alternatives to force have been exhausted and UN Security Council authorization for the use of force cannot be secured. When such a case arises, states should evaluate possible courses of preventive action based on standards of international legitimacy.

Some argue against using the concept of legitimacy to evaluate the use of force on the grounds that its criteria are broad, subjective, and too permissive and so its application would undermine current international law. But relying on legitimacy is unlikely to result in less adherence to international law, since the current use-of-force rules are already routinely disregarded as impractical or unsound. Other critics argue that the notion of legitimacy is no more likely to govern the use of force effectively than are current legal standards. But the utility of legitimacy lies, partly, in the modesty of its claims. Unlike traditional legal arguments, which purport to rely on established rules to vindicate or condemn state behavior, arguments based on legitimacy claim only to guide complicated decision making by subjecting that process to a survey of the full range of relevant international opinion.

States have much to gain and little, if anything, to lose by subjecting their decisions to use preventive (or other) force to systematic legitimacy tests. Encouraging such disciplined examination should enhance the prospect that states will use preventive force in ways consistent with the goals of the UN charter—and that their actions will, thanks to the international support they receive, stand a greater chance of succeeding. A state that disregards this process, on the other hand, is more likely to fail, or to pay higher costs in achieving its objectives.

> *"Justification of preventive war is by its nature counterfactual; in other words, it is based on events that did not occur. . . . But just because counterfactual historic arguments are inherently controversial, it does not mean they are never valid."*

Preventive War Can Be Valid Even If It Cannot Be Justified

Peter Hetherington

In the following viewpoint, author Peter Hetherington argues that preventive war may be necessary in order to counter threats that could potentially bring about more serious consequences if left unchecked. Hetherington uses the example of Polish states-man Joseph Pilsudski (Józef Piłsudski), a patriot who feared Eu-ropean powers would sacrifice his country to Nazi Germany if Adolf Hitler's aggression was not restrained. Hetherington states that Pilsudski tried to find allies to launch a preventive strike against Germany, but both England and France—the powers that fought Germany only a few decades earlier—declined to participate. Although Hetherington admits that no one can be sure if preventive war will be effective or even justifiable because

Peter Hetherington, "Is Preventive War Ever Justified?," *Huffington Post*, July 5, 2012.

it seeks to preempt an assumed wrongdoing, he attests that in the case of Pilsudski's prediction, a preventive act against Hitler's regime may have spared Europe the ravages of World War II. Hetherington is the author of Unvanquished: Joseph Pilsudski, Resurrected Poland and the Struggle for Eastern Europe.

As you read, consider the following questions:

1. Why does Hetherington maintain that in 1933 Poland may have been able to make good on a preventive attack on Germany?

2. What was Britain's reaction to Pilsudski's overtures for a concerted preventive attack on Nazi Germany, according to Hetherington?

3. In what year did Joseph Pilsudski die, as Hetherington states?

The wisdom of preventive war, or military action designed to eliminate a threat before it materializes, has been a subject of intense debate. Was the war in Iraq justified? And of more immediate concern, is an Israeli military strike against Iran [because of Iran's intention of becoming a nuclear power] advisable?

The arguments against preventive war are compelling. These actions rely on accurate intelligence concerning the intentions and capabilities of the targeted state. It is a dangerous precedent—potentially destabilizing—and has been used to mask ulterior motives or to justify aggression.

The Nazi Threat During World War II

Despite these objections, at least one case for preventive war is worthy of consideration. In 1933, Adolf Hitler became chancellor of Germany. Since he had openly declared his desire to repudiate the Versailles Treaty, rearm Germany, and seize land necessary for German "living space," it was not unreasonable to assume that the Nazi regime was intent on military conquest. Yet as soon as he gained power, Hitler began preaching peace. At international forums, the Germans proclaimed they were only seeking equality with fellow nations, and that as soon as their legitimate grievances were adjudicated, they would live peacefully with their neighbors.

Although Hitler had made numerous statements to the contrary, the Great Powers (Britain and France) were fearful of provoking Germany. Rather than point out contradictions and blatant treaty violations, they preferred to be officially ignorant of obvious facts. Instead of collective resolve, Hitler was treated to appeasement, a policy that allowed him to advance preparations for what would be the greatest tragedy in history.

However, one prominent European statesman not only recognized the Nazi threat, but was also determined to do something about it. Józef Pilsudski, the leader of the Polish state, had ample experience with the aggressive tendencies of his neighbors. Germany and Russia had conspired to partition Poland in 1795, leading to over a century of enslavement before the country was liberated in the aftermath of WWI [World War I]. For well over a decade, Pilsudski had seen Europe's collective security system erode, and noticed that his ostensive allies were becoming increasingly willing to abandon Poland to avoid conflict with Germany.

Having observed countless international conferences where German demands were satisfied, only to be met with new delays and grievances, he recognized that the Nazi regime was not acting in good faith. He knew Germany was bent on regaining her "lost" Polish lands. Pilsudski believed Hitler was pursuing what appeared to be peaceful policies as a means of advancing his revisionist agenda only because he lacked, for the time being, the military means to accomplish his goals. Ultimately, the Nazi threat could only be stopped by force, or at least the credible threat of force. Pilsudski was not opposed to peaceful resolutions; he just doubted they were possible in this case, and viewed an attack on Germany as a justifiable defense of the Polish state.

Pilsudski's Preventive War

Recognizing that Hitler was immune to normal diplomacy, Pilsudski began preparations for a preventive war. Unlike the situation in 1939, in March 1933, Poland was in a position to carry out this threat. As Hitler knew, the Polish army possessed more than 250,000 highly trained and well-equipped soldiers. Although in the initial stages of secretly rearming, in 1933 the German military had no modern weapons, namely airplanes, tanks, or armored cars, and according to the terms of the Versailles Treaty its army was limited to 100,000 men. Pilsudski was prepared to send Polish troops to occupy Danzig, East Prussia, and possibly Upper Silesia, while France would march through the Rhineland into the Ruhr. The move would expose the weakness of the boisterous young Nazi regime, humiliate Hitler, and possibly remove him from power. The occupying troops would then refuse to evacuate German territory until the Reich made assurances to honor the peace treaty.

While the details are murky due to his preference for secret diplomacy, according to some reports Pilsudski made this proposal on several occasions to the French, but was repeatedly rebuffed. France would not act without Britain, and the British not only refused to participate, but intimated they might support Germany if Poland was determined the aggressor.

In the end, the preventive war against Germany never materialized. But Pilsudski, who had defeated the Red Army without Western assistance in 1920, was apparently prepared to ignore international consensus and order unilateral action to defend the Polish state. Significantly, Hitler—who understood Pilsudski was not prone to issue empty threats—believed this to be true. Poland used the threat of preventive war to maneuver Germany into a series of agreements designed to buy time to prepare for the inevitable war Pilsudski saw coming.

Unfortunately, the Polish leader died in 1935. Poland, which had lost its brief military superiority, was attacked and overwhelmed by Germany in 1939. It will never be known if Pilsudski's preventive war could have eliminated the Nazi threat. What is known is that without it, millions of Poles were killed and the survivors condemned to another half century of enslavement.

Preventive War as an Option to Deter More Tragic Consequences

Justification of preventive war is by its nature counterfactual; in other words, it is based on events that did not occur. Such action is perhaps particularly difficult to justify if it's successful. By definition, the original threat would have been eliminated. But just because counterfactual historic arguments are inherently controversial, it does not mean they are never valid. One can make the reasonable case that preventive war against Hitler in 1933 would have altered history in a positive direction and might have spared Europe from the nightmare of WWII [World War II].

Preventive military action should be viewed with a healthy skepticism and used as a measured response to a defined imminent threat. It goes without saying that it should only be used after reasonable diplomatic efforts have failed. But just as in the case of Germany in 1933, the consequences of failure in Iran today are enormous and warrant keeping all options— even preventive war—on the table.

> *"The burden of a clear and eminent threat of attack [from Iraq or Afghanistan] was and remains unsupported by the evidence. This is a violation of international law and just war theory."*

US Wars in Iraq and Afghanistan Are Unjust

Ryan King

Ryan King argues in the following viewpoint that the US wars in Iraq and Afghanistan are unjust under the principles of just war theory—a collection of guidelines that have their origins in ancient Roman and Catholic philosophy. According to King, "just wars" are fought in self-defense and after other attempts at resolution have failed. He maintains that the United States did not invade Iraq and Afghanistan out of self-defense, nor had Washington exhausted other means of achieving a peaceful solution to the looming conflicts. Instead, King asserts that the presidential administration of George W. Bush turned on Afghanistan when its rulers refused to hand over terrorist leader Osama bin Laden and then attacked Iraq "presumably" to secure its oil reserves. Neither course of action, King contends, follows the precepts of a just war, thus revealing that Bush's administration acted out of economic and political self-interest. Ryan King is a writer whose work appears on Daily Censored, *an online forum for topics that are commonly censored in various media outlets.*

As you read, consider the following questions:

1. As King reports, what former Iraqi foreign minister (and paid informant) confirmed that his country did not possess weapons of mass destruction (WMD) prior to the US-led invasion?

2. Why does King assert that the wars in Iraq and Afghanistan could not conceivably meet the "high probability of success" standard that pertains to just war theory?

3. After forces failed to find WMD in Iraq, what does King claim the Bush administration adopted as a new justification for invading that country?

In any war the only justifiable cause of warfare is to defend oneself or to defend others, according to just war theory. For the Iraq war, the primary justification to invade was on the grounds of self-defense. Former president [George W.] Bush, along with many other government officials, told the country and the world that America must use "anticipatory self-defense" to protect the nation from an attack at home. The primary reason given was that the administration believed Iraq had and was developing weapons of mass destruction (WMD) and that it planned to use those WMD against the United States, probably by the proxy of the terrorist organizations they believed Iraq supported.

Self-defense is unanimously justified as a cause of war in . . . the just war theory. . . . However, anticipatory self-defense is not as clearly justified. International law, which the just war theory requires adherence to, is not. [Former national security advisor and secretary of state] Condoleezza Rice outlined the Bush administration's view of "anticipatory self-defense" as "the right of the United States to attack a country that *it thinks* could attack it first." By this definition [the terrorist group] al-Qaeda and the Taliban were merely conducting "anticipatory self-defense" when they attacked the World Trade Center on September 11, 2001. This is so because Osama bin Laden and the Taliban received threats of possible American military strikes against them two months before the terrorist assaults on New York and Washington. Also the White House was given comprehensive plans to conduct an offensive to "rid the world of al-Qaeda" just days before the September 11th attacks. This conclusion would be absolutely outrageous to both the Bush administration and the American people.

No Justification for War Against Iraq

International law states that for "anticipatory self-defense" to be justified the threat must be imminent and the burden of proof is on the country pushing to strike first to provide sufficient evidence of this threat. The U.S. simply could not provide sufficient evidence that Iraq was developing WMD and was intending to use them against the U.S. However, there was quite a bit of evidence that suggested otherwise. The reason for this disparity, of course, as the world soon learned, was that Iraq stopped development of its nuclear, chemical and biological weapons programs back in 1991 in accordance with international law. So it is clear that the grounds for "anticipatory self-defense" against Iraq were not sufficient for the just war theory, nor did the U.S. have the authority to make these decisions. . . .

In the Downing Street memo, a note of a secret meeting of British government figures, the head of the Secret Intelligence Service describes what he learned from a recent visit to Washington: "Bush wanted to remove Saddam Hussein, through military action, justified by the conjunction of terrorism and WMD. But the intelligence and facts were being fixed around the policy." The United Nations Monitoring, Verification and Inspection Commission in March 2003, just days before the invasion of Iraq, stated that it "did not find evidence of the continuation or resumption of programmes of weapons of mass destruction." Naji Sabri, Iraq's foreign minister, who was part of Hussein's inner circle and was being paid by the French as an agent, confirmed that Iraq did not have WMD. Two senior CIA [U.S. Central Intelligence Agency] officers approved this intelligence and President Bush was briefed on this info on September 18th 2002. Bush dismissed this intelligence and failed to share it with Congress or the CIA agents investigating whether Hussein had WMD. According to national security and intelligence analyst John Prados, in a review of the documentary record, the Bush administration knew that Iraqi WMD programs "were either nascent, moribund or non-existent—exactly the opposite of the president's repeated message to Americans." If Prados is correct then the Bush administration falsified intelligence to justify "anticipatory self-defense." In such a case, the U.S. would then simply be aggressors in an unjustifiable war. Presumably the cause of this war is to control the world's second largest known oil reserve (a view shared by the majority of Iraqis in Baghdad). The cause of this war then would be to increase the country's power. This cause is not justified by the just war theory. . . .

Just Wars Are Undertaken When Other Alternatives Are Exhausted

The second cause given for the war in Iraq and the main cause for the war in Afghanistan was to end terrorism. This is again an argument of self-defense. The thinking goes: We are attacked by terrorists, like the September 11th attacks, so we must destroy these terrorist organizations, such as al-Qaeda and the Taliban, who harbor them. On the surface this seems like justifiable self-defense. The U.S. must be able to show that terrorist organizations pose an imminent threat to the U.S. The U.S. used the September 11th attacks as evidence; thus, the U.S. could show that terrorist organizations, namely al-

Qaeda, posed an eminent threat. However, this terrorist organization is not a country; it is an organization that the U.S. believed was harbored by the state, the Taliban. Let us assume the Taliban harbored al-Qaeda; again, normally a heavy burden of proof would be on the U.S. to produce evidence both that al-Qaeda conducted the September 11th attacks and the Taliban harbored al-Qaeda.... The U.S. then demanded that the Taliban hand over the leader of al-Qaeda, Osama bin Laden. The Taliban said it would comply if the U.S. would give them evidence linking bin Laden with the September 11th attacks. The U.S. rejected the offer. Then the Taliban offered to try bin Laden under Islamic law; again, the Bush administration rejected the offer stating, "There will be no negotiations." The U.S. flatly rejected a judicial and diplomatic possible solution in Iraq. The U.S. subsequently invaded Iraq with aims of destroying al-Qaeda and the Taliban and capturing bin Laden. The U.S. violated the clause in just war theory of last resort, which states force may only be used after all peaceful and viable alternatives have been seriously tried and exhausted.... While the threat of terrorism is very real and there are grounds to justify war by way of the self-defense clause, the fact that the U.S. did not exhaust, or even attempt peaceful methods of decreasing this threat first, means that the U.S. is not justified by the just war theory.....

No High Probability of Success

For a war to be ethical in the just war theory ... there must be a high probability of success. There was hardly a doubt that U.S. military forces could topple the Taliban and al-Qaeda forces in Iraq and Afghanistan. However, there was considerable doubt about the war's ability to end or even reduce terrorism. This is a stated cause of war, so accordingly it must have a high probability of success to be just. As these wars have continued, it has become quite clear that they have not ended or reduced terrorism. In fact, as predicted since the

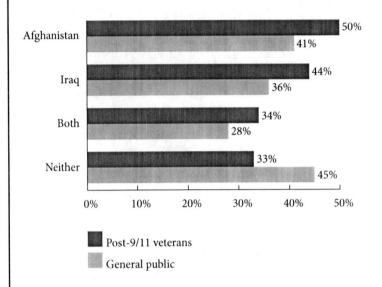

Veterans and Civilians Slightly Differ on War Opinion

Percentage that say Afghanistan or Iraq wars were worth fighting.

Afghanistan: Post-9/11 veterans 50%, General public 41%
Iraq: Post-9/11 veterans 44%, General public 36%
Both: Post-9/11 veterans 34%, General public 28%
Neither: Post-9/11 veterans 33%, General public 45%

■ Post-9/11 veterans
▨ General public

TAKEN FROM: Pew Research Center, "War and Sacrifice in the Post-9/11 Era," October 5, 2011.

development of these wars, the world and the U.S. have seen considerably more terrorism than before these wars. Many top U.S. officials believe that these wars caused the increase in terrorism the world is experiencing. Most U.S. troops think we should leave Iraq, 72%, according to a Zogby International poll. Many terrorists themselves list grievances caused by the U.S. wars in Iraq and Afghanistan as the reason they conducted terrorist activity. One recent example is Najibullah Zazi, a member of al-Qaeda, who recently pleaded guilty to plotting to blow up a subway system. Zazi confessed that he planned this attack to "sacrifice myself to bring attention to what the United States military was doing to civilian[s] in Afghanistan by sacrificing my soul for the sake of saving other souls." According to a RAND study, most U.S. analysts on the ground in Iraq and Afghanistan believe that terrorism is increasing because of U.S. troops in Iraq and Afghanistan, and they support a U.S. withdrawal. According to polls, 45% of the population of Iraq now views terrorism against the U.S. favorably. This shows that the probability of success, in reducing or eliminating terrorism, is not only extremely low, but most probably negative. This is a violation of the just war theory clause that wars must have a high probability of success. . . .

No Proof of WMD in Iraq Leads Bush to Change His Justification for War

The Defense Intelligence Agency and the CIA concluded that Saddam Hussein did not support al-Qaeda. The CIA in January 2003 concluded that Hussein "viewed Islamic extremists operating inside Iraq as a threat." In February 2002 the Defense Intelligence Agency concluded that "Iraq is unlikely to have provided bin Laden any useful [chemical and biological weapons] knowledge or assistance." A year later Bush said: "Iraq has also provided al-Qaeda with chemical and biological weapons training." This calls into question Iraq's alleged connection to al-Qaeda, one of the causes given for the invasion. Under international law and just war theory the burden of proof was upon the Bush administration to provide convincing evidence that Iraq posed a danger to the U.S. by supporting terrorism against the U.S., as the Bush administration claimed. This convincing evidence was and remains virtually nonexistent, in the face of much counterevidence. Rex Tomb, chief of investigative publicity for the FBI [Federal Bureau of Investigation], informs us that the FBI has no hard evidence connecting bin Laden to the September 11th attacks; a premise the Bush administration relied on to invade Iraq. The burden of a clear and eminent threat of attack was and remains unsupported by the evidence. This is a violation of international law and just war theory. It also undermines the entire premise of self-defense as a cause for the Iraq and Afghanistan wars. . . .

Shortly after it was clear that Iraq did not have any WMD, President Bush and his administration started to state that our mission in Iraq and Afghanistan was to bring democracy to these countries. The spread of democracy was supported by the Bush administration as a way to liberate the people of Iraq and Afghanistan from the tyrannical rule they were subject to. The timing of this shift in political rhetoric should bring the administration's motives into question. The people of Iraq were indeed suspicious of their motives. A Gallup poll conducted in October 2003 asked the people of Baghdad why they thought the U.S. invaded Iraq; 1% felt the goal was to bring democracy and 5% thought the goal was to assist the Iraqi people. The large majority thought that the U.S. sought to rob Iraq of its oil.

To spread democracy by liberating a people from tyrannical rule can be seen as an act of humanitarian intervention, which is supported by the just war theory. However, the U.S. is not consistent in its support for democracy abroad. Thomas Carothers, director of the Democracy and Rule of Law project at the Carnegie Endowment [for International Peace], reviewed the U.S. record of democracy promotion since the Cold War [a period of tension between the United States and the Soviet Union during the second half of the twentieth century]. Carothers found "where democracy appears to fit in well with US security and economic interests, the United States promotes democracy. Where democracy clashes with other significant interests, it is downplayed or even ignored."

The U.S. did not want democratic elections to take place in Iraq, probably because the Iraqi people wanted the U.S. out of Iraq. Dr. Alan Richards, UC [University of California] Santa Cruz professor and Middle East scholar, points out that the U.S. "initially opposed early elections in Iraq, after Ayatollah Sistani turned huge numbers of his followers out in the streets to demand such elections, Washington had little choice but to agree." They also made sure there was no freedom of press before the elections by bombing Al Jazeera, a television network that was distinctly anti-American. . . .

We have . . . examined criteria of the just war theory . . . on the cause of war (*jus ad bellum*) including just cause, last resort, and high probability of success. In each case, we have found that the current U.S. wars in Iraq and Afghanistan fail to meet any of these criteria.

> *"There are no guarantees that a risky enterprise such as the Afghanistan war will become just. But we do not have to be ethically tone deaf, either."*

The United States Can and Should Seek to Justify Its War in Afghanistan

Susan Brooks Thistlethwaite and Brian Katulis

In the following viewpoint, Susan Brooks Thistlethwaite and Brian Katulis insist that President Barack Obama should give a moral purpose to the ongoing war in Afghanistan. In the authors' opinion, the president should bring the war back under the precepts of just war theory, a set of principles that outline justifications for warfare. According to Thistlethwaite and Katulis, US involvement in Afghanistan can be justified if it is waged to ensure stability in the region and if it has achievable goals. In this light, America must employ more than just military force to bring peace to the region, and it must do its best to protect the civilian population from harm, the authors assert. Finally, President Obama should work with the international community, Thistlethwaite and Katulis contend, to clarify US aims and to garner a collective moral sanction for the continued operation in Afghanistan. Susan Brooks Thistlethwaite is an ordained minister of the United Church of Christ, a professor of theology at Chicago Theological Seminary, and a senior fellow at the Center for American Progress, a progressive educational institute. Brian Katulis is a senior fellow at the Center for American Progress.

As you read, consider the following questions:

1. Why do Thistlethwaite and Katulis believe that President Obama should return to Congress for a reauthorization of the war?

2. Why do the authors think it would be valuable to work with Pakistan, Saudi Arabia, and the United Arab Emirates in developing peaceful solutions to problems in Afghanistan?

3. What do the authors claim was the human rights hallmark of success for the George W. Bush administration's intervention in Afghanistan?

Moral considerations have been largely absent from our country's public debate over what to do in Afghanistan. The [Barack] Obama administration has been working since Afghanistan's August [2009] elections to refine its goals, assess the intentions of key countries such as Pakistan, and gain additional commitments from allies in NATO [North Atlantic Treaty Organization].

The focus on troop levels and money is important, but the debate has been insufficient and limited. It is not too late to raise moral questions regarding the war in Afghanistan. Indeed, these criteria can help refine the revised strategy for Afghanistan. It was to America's detriment that the previous administration often eschewed established moral theory or based its policy decisions on a simplistic and distorted worldview of "good" versus "evil."

Just War Theory and the War in Afghanistan

There are two broad considerations in just war theory. First, whether it is just to go to war at all. And second, how force may and may not be used. There must be a just cause and a legitimate authority. War must be a last resort, and there should be a probability of success. Military forces must limit the use of force and protect noncombatants, and there has to be a good outcome, including an exit strategy.

The war in Afghanistan is especially taxing for this theory. The Afghanistan war is now well into its ninth year—longer than America's involvement in last century's two world wars combined. The original justification has been overtaken by events, and some operations—such as air strikes killing a disproportionate number of civilians—have made it difficult to classify Afghanistan as a just war.

Some would even argue that it is a reach to think that the war in Afghanistan could become just. These critics are not wholly wrong. It is well to remember the insight of one of the 20th century's premier thinkers on just war: Reinhold Niebuhr. One of the biggest problems of American foreign policy, Niebuhr contended, is that Americans are tempted to overreach, to overestimate the innocence of our own power, and thus also overestimate its possible effectiveness.

But for that reason alone, it is all the more important for the administration to ask larger moral questions and use theory to examine policy considerations. There are no guarantees that a risky enterprise such as the Afghanistan war will become just. But we do not have to be ethically tone deaf, either.

Within this just war framework, the Obama administration can take steps to move forward by critically engaging moral considerations in regard to substantial policy changes. And just war theory may just have to evolve again to meet the challenge the Afghanistan war presents.

Utilizing Just War Theory to Shape Decisions on Afghanistan Policy

The Obama administration's review should move beyond resources and tactics to a broader reflection on the justness of the cause, which can help bring greater clarity to the goals of the mission. With Americans sending their family members into harm's way, it is particularly important for the administration to bring morality regarding the conduct of the war into the dialogue. Just war considerations are directly relevant to prospects for security, peace, and justice in Afghanistan—and reflecting on the key criteria can point to specific actions the Obama administration could take.

1. Just cause. Force is reasonable according to just war theory if it is in defense against aggression, or in the protection of the vulnerable or allies.

The original justification for going to war in Afghanistan—defending against the aggression of the September 11th [2001] attacks—had broad global support. That support has waned at home and abroad as the nature of the threat has changed from a non-state actor with a base in Afghanistan to a global network that has dispersed into Pakistan and around the world. There is a moral argument for continued efforts in Afghanistan in order to enhance regional stability—South Asia has two nuclear powers—India and Pakistan—and increased tensions and instability in this part of the world could have major implications for global security.

Obama should return to Congress for a renewed authorization for the Afghanistan war. The initial authorization of the war is largely outdated, but the administration can, and should, make a strong case for additional resources and renewed focus based on the global security interests and need for stability in the broader region. The symbolism of a renewed commitment would help move beyond the notion of endless war that has been perpetuated by relying on supplemental funding mechanisms each year that have not offered an opportunity for renewed and broader public debate on the issue.

President Obama should also consider returning to the United Nations [U.N.] Security Council to renew and update the resolutions guiding the U.S. and NATO presence in Afghanistan. The current language is broad and lacks a clear focus. And it is essential as the administration makes changes to its policy on Afghanistan that there is deliberation with the bodies that can help address the moral question of intention in regard to this war.

These two steps are not necessary from a legal standpoint, but the public debate could help further define how the war in Afghanistan is a just cause—seeking to advance regional stability, prevent the escalation of regional tensions, and perhaps even reaffirm basic rights enshrined in the U.N. [Universal] Declaration of Human Rights.

2. Right authority. Only a legitimate government, or internationally recognized authority such as the United Nations, can conduct war. Revisiting the authorization in Congress and at the United Nations can help address a second consideration of just war theory—the right authority. But another set of actions—focused on Afghan governing authorities—is also necessary to effectively address the question.

The international community is working to obtain a more concrete set of commitments from Afghanistan's leadership to deal with the problems that have undermined the Afghan government's legitimacy: namely corruption, weak governance, and poor performance on providing justice. Working to boost the full range of Afghan institutions—the national, provincial, and local levels of government—is central to the effort to help achieve sustainable security in Afghanistan and address the insurgency that has been raging in many parts of the country. What some pundits have categorized as "dithering" has actually been essential to regaining leverage to shape the strategic calculations and actions of Afghanistan's leaders, who have a feeble record of providing their citizens with basic needs.

3. Last resort. A country must exhaust all other reasonable means before using military action. The Obama administration has had extensive consultations with allies in Europe, key powers such as Russia and China, and important regional actors such as Pakistan and India. This has been one part of making sure that no diplomatic stone is left unturned. Secretary of State Hillary Clinton and U.S. special representative for Afghanistan and Pakistan Richard Holbrooke have logged in thousands of miles in trips as part of consultations with other countries—all part of a broader effort to develop a coordinated strategy with stronger support for all operations in Afghanistan, including military operations necessary to stabilize key parts of the country.

Making sure that military operations in certain parts of Afghanistan are a last resort also requires the United States and other members of the coalition to test whether there are alternative means—including political, diplomatic, and economic ways—to deal with elements of the insurgency in Afghanistan. Using the other elements of America's power could help reshape the calculations of some Taliban leaders and motivate them to drop their weapons. Working with countries such as Pakistan, Saudi Arabia, and the United Arab Emirates—all of whom have extensive contacts with Taliban leadership—could be a way of developing peaceful alternatives to addressing instability in Afghanistan.

4. Probability of success. It is unjust to wage war if defeat is the most likely outcome. The nature of the war in Afghanistan means that U.S. military forces cannot achieve success on their own—the struggle for stability is not purely a conventional military struggle. It requires collective action by countries in South Asia and support from other countries.

It also requires a stronger effort to help Afghan institutions address the population's basic needs—security, economic development, and justice. The renewed effort to send additional resources and expertise through a "civilian surge" of diplomats and development specialists is aimed at increasing the probability of success in what is an asymmetrical war against non-state actors.

5. *Proportionality.* Force must be limited by goals; noncombatants should be protected from harm and never targeted. Security and safety for Afghan women must be a central and not a peripheral consideration in a changed policy. The previous administration made the "liberation" of women from the harsh rule of the Taliban a hallmark of its "success." But the human rights situation for many women in Afghanistan never lived up to this hype, and their physical, social, and civic security has worsened over time.

Making the population's safety and security central to the mission—something that General Stanley McChrystal has argued—will require a different mode of operating, and it will raise tough questions about certain tactics employed by the United States and its NATO allies such as unmanned aerial drone strikes. The proportionality question is deeply complicated by the nature of the threats posed by non-state actors and insurgencies and raises thorny questions for just war theory. But evaluating more closely the military tactics employed in efforts to stabilize Afghanistan and the broader region can help bring greater moral clarity to the mission.

6. *Good outcome.* Force should be limited in scope with a definite end, and there should be no extended warfare. President Obama needs to outline an exit strategy with perhaps even a clear date for completion, understanding that dates can slip. One dangerous thought that has crept into our dialogue is the notion of the "long war" or the war without end. Changing the mind-set on national security requires the Obama ad-

ministration to do something its predecessor was reluctant to do—offer a light at the end of the tunnel in the efforts to stabilize volatile areas of the world.

Afghanistan's Challenge to Just War Theory

The war in Afghanistan raises crucial questions for just war theory, not the least of which is whether just war criteria can be used to change course in a war that is already more than eight years long. Can the cause of an ongoing conflict become more just, for example, and exactly how could that happen? Can diplomacy come to play an increasing role in an ongoing conflict, and if so, does that redefine last resort?

The rise of nation-states posed a challenge to the evolution of just war theory, as did the dawn of the nuclear age. And now we must consider whole regions and non-state actors, rather than just individual states. This adds difficulties, but it also adds options.

Questions of just cause become more acute, for example, when major regional players possess nuclear weapons. But a greater regional focus also allows other states, and entities within a state, to become diplomatic agents, perhaps reducing the need to use force at all.

The regional approach also redefines the probability of success. A positive vision for a given region helps prevent actions that suppress conflict in one country only to destabilize another. Recognizing and dealing with the reality of all parties in a conflict, state and non-state actors alike, helps create more permanent solutions. It also allows crucial attention to be paid to the lives of those most affected by conflict, and those who will be affected if an unjust and unstable peace is the outcome.

Recognizing global security interests in the world today requires partners, and it demands that we expand the understanding of "right authority" to include an assessment of the "rightness" of our partner states. Do they have legitimate authority, and how do they exercise that authority?

As President Obama makes his decisions on the next steps in the Afghanistan war, he should take care to weigh these broader moral questions in his deliberations in order to increase the chances for progress towards peace and justice in that troubled region.

Periodical Bibliography

The following articles have been selected to supplement the diverse views presented in this chapter.

Talal Asad
"Thinking About Terrorism and Just War," *Cambridge Review of International Affairs*, March 2010.

Onder Bakircioglu
"The Future of Preventive Wars: The Case of Iraq," *Third World Quarterly*, October 2009.

Khalid Yahya Blankinship
"Parity of Muslim and Western Concepts of Just War," *Muslim World*, July 2011.

Robert J. Delahunty and John Yoo
"The 'Bush Doctrine': Can Preventive War Be Justified?," *Harvard Journal of Law & Public Policy*, Summer 2009.

Andrew Fiala
"Crusades, Just Wars, and the Bush Doctrine," *Peace Review*, June 2007.

David Fisher and Nigel Biggar
"Was Iraq an Unjust War? A Debate on the Iraq War and Reflections on Libya," *International Affairs*, May 2011.

Doug McCready
"Ending the War Right: *Jus Post Bellum* and the Just War Tradition," *Journal of Military Ethics*, March 2009.

Thomas W. McShane
"In Search of the Good War," *Military Review*, September/October 2012.

David Mellow
"Iraq: A Morally Justified Resort to War," *Journal of Applied Philosophy*, August 2006.

Cian O'Driscoll
"Talking About Just War: Obama in Oslo, Bush at War," *Politics*, June 2011.

OPPOSING
VIEWPOINTS®
SERIES

CHAPTER 2

What Will Likely Be the Causes of Future Wars?

Chapter Preface

In July 2007, a Russian nuclear submarine drilled a hole through the ice cap in the Arctic Ocean in order to permit two smaller underwater vehicles to descend into the frigid depths and plant a titanium flag on the seabed below the North Pole. The intent of the mission was to claim the area for Russian energy exploration. Moscow insisted it was within its rights to make such a claim because the region is linked to the Siberian continental plate. The seabed in the region is thought to hold a quarter of the world's untapped oil and natural gas reserves, and Russian president Vladimir Putin wanted to make sure other nations recognized Russia's right to extract these resources if and when deep-sea drilling in such an inhospitable environment proved feasible.

Other countries that share a border with the Arctic such as the United States, Canada, Norway, and Denmark (through Greenland) dismissed such territorializing. In a July 31, 2007, ABC News article, David Rivkin Jr., a maritime law expert who served in the US Departments of Justice and Energy, stated, "Russia has always employed a muscular rhetoric that doesn't necessarily mean anything. Planting a flag somewhere doesn't make it your territory." Nations that prove their continental shelf connects to Arctic ridges can also press such claims. Both Canada and Denmark immediately expressed their rights over Arctic territories and showed contempt for a statement made by the Russian expedition's leader, Artur Chilingarov, that "the Arctic is Russian."

Over the next few years, Russia pressed its claim while investing in upgrades to its Northern Fleet. Some observers feared what a lack of resolution might bring. For example, in 2008, Jane's Information Group, a British open-source intelligence organization focusing on military policy and conflict, made a somewhat expected prediction in light of the retreat of Arctic ice due to warming global temperatures. "This retreat has led to territorial claims, raising the possibility of a genuinely cold war between Western states and Russia over the disputed Arctic region," Jane's asserted. Then, in 2010, Putin, at the time Russia's prime minster under President Dmitry Medvedev, softened the "muscular rhetoric," asserting that he hoped the United Nations could foster some rulings on cooperation in the region. At an international Arctic conference in Moscow, he remarked, "If you stand alone you can't survive in the Arctic. Nature makes people and states to help each other." He began canvassing for foreign investment and foreign technology to help unlock the oil and gas reserves. At the same time, Chilingarov was sent off on another mission to study the region in depth and verify Russia's claims.

Though Putin pledges a peaceful division of the untapped spoils for those nations with claimant rights, a series of North Atlantic Treaty Organization (NATO) military exercises involving sixteen thousand troops and several warships along the northern edges of Norway and Sweden in March 2012 suggested that the West was still acting cautiously. Immediately, Igor Korotchenko, a national security analyst and chairman of the public advisory council to Russia's Ministry of Defense, told the Voice of Russia radio service that "Russia is creating two Arctic mobile brigades which will ensure effective operations in any part of the Arctic." The Voice of Russia, though, affirmed that Moscow was still dedicated to a diplomatic resolution.

The rush for energy resources is one anticipated cause of future global conflict discussed in the following chapter. Scarcity has on occasion led nations to rattle sabers and vie for control of energy stocks as well as other vital resources needed to keep nations running. However, as several of the chapter viewpoints insist, identifying such triggers can also lead to cooler heads and preventive agreements to avert warfare.

> *"Of the 263 international waterways in the world, all are managed more or less peacefully."*

The Threat of Future Water Wars Is Exaggerated

Thomas Lawfield

Thomas Lawfield is a graduate student at the University for Peace, an academic institution established in Costa Rica by a United Nations mandate. In the following viewpoint, he debunks claims that water scarcity is a concern that would lead to future armed conflicts. Indeed, Lawfield insists that throughout history disputes over water supplies have led to agreements between nations that advocate sharing the resource. Lawfield believes that countries have more to lose by going to war over water than they would have by cooperating to provide access to all. This, he concludes, should indicate to observers that water sharing is helping reduce the potential for conflict in the world.

As you read, consider the following questions:

1. According to Lawfield, who fought the only known water war in world history?

Thomas Lawfield, "Water Security: War or Peace?," *Peace & Conflict Monitor Special Report*, May 3, 2010. Copyright © 2010 by Peace & Conflict Monitor. All rights reserved. Reproduced by permission.

2. Why does the author believe it would be illogical for Israel to go to war with Palestine over the water resources of the West Bank?

3. How many water-related treaties have been signed between the years 805 and 1984, as Lawfield reports?

The water war thesis comes from a strong political pedigree. A number of key state heads in the Middle East and North Africa have made significant claims linking water and conflict. For instance, President Anwar Sadat of Egypt in 1979: 'The only matter that could take Egypt to war again is water.' Likewise, former UN [United Nations] Secretary-General [Boutros] Boutros-Ghali pointed out that the 'national security of Egypt . . . is a question of water.' Such sentiments have been echoed by two more recent secretary-generals who have commented that 'if we are not careful, future wars are going to be about water and not oil' with a likelihood of 'transforming peaceful competition into violence.'

Such populist talk is matched by an attendant academic literature linking conflict and water in a state of 'emergency.' Some approaches look for a statistical correlation between the existence of international water courses and conflict. [In a 2001 *Foreign Policy* article, Sandra L. Postel and Aaron T. Wolf point] out: 'One fourth of water-related interactions during the last half century were hostile.' In particular, these authors look for the existence of increased water stress (induced by population growth) and conflict. This focus operates on the assumption that the greater the need for water, the greater the stakes that the state is willing to place on securing access to the water resource. As Postel [and Wolf make] clear: 'The unprecedented degree of current water stress is creating more zero-sum situations both within and between countries.' This gives a certain logical predictability to the trajectory of water conflicts—suggesting a direct correlation between those sites where there is a shortage of water and the incidence of conflict.

Such 'irrefutable evidence' takes on a highly geographical nature, where particular river basins and hydrological typologies are established as potential sites of conflict, such as in the case of the Middle East and North Africa, where the Nile and Jordan/Israel examples have emerged as a central flagship example for future war, conflict and instability induced by water scarcity. [Postel and Wolf's article] confidently proclaims [according to Joyce R. Starr in a 1991 *Foreign Policy* article] that 'the largest and most combustible imbalance between population and available water supplies will be in Asia.' In addition, another report selects seventeen shared river basins and dam instances distributed globally where conflict is likely to occur.

Causal Explanations Explained

Explaining why water causes conflict has been straightforward—an explanation which reflects [as Postel and Wolf claim] a 'heightened competition for [*finite*] water between cities and farms, between neighbouring states and provinces, and at times between nations.'

The causal explanation for such a link suggests that increased stress on the water resource occurs in two planes: an increase in demand, and/or a decrease in supply. Some authors place more weight on the argument that population growth (demand increase) will be the cause, while others prefer a decline in supply explanation, such as the expectation that water availability per capita is expected to decline by twenty per cent by 2025. . . . Both scenarios induce stress on the water resource and link natural and human systems in a highly interdependent and mutually vulnerable relationship. The conflict scenario occurs when an attempt is made to maintain or increase supply to meet demand in a situation where demand is either static or increasing. . . .

There Is No Water Crisis

In reality, water does not cause war. The arguments presented above, although correct in principle, have little purchase in empirical evidence. Indeed, as one author notes, there is only one case of a war where the formal declaration of war was over water. This was an incident between two Mesopotamian city states, Lagash and Umma, over 2,500 years BC, in modern-day southern Iraq. . . .

Why then is water not a cause of war? The answer lies in two factors: *first*, the capacity for adaptation to water stresses and, *second*, the political drawbacks to coupling water and conflict.

First, there is no water crisis, or more correctly, there are a number of adaptation strategies that reduce stress on water resources and so make conflict less likely. Unlike the water war discourse, which perceives water as finite in the Malthusian sense[1], the capacity for adaptation to water stress has been greatly underestimated. For instance, I will discuss in particular a trading adaptation known as 'virtual water', which refers to the water used to grow imported food. This water can be subtracted from the total projected agricultural water needs of a state, and hence allows water-scarce states to operate on a lower in-country water requirement than would otherwise be expected. This means that regions of the world that are particularly rich in water produce water-intense agricultural products more easily in the global trade system, while other water-scarce areas produce low-intensity products. The scale of this water is significant—[social scientist Tony] Allan famously pointed out that more embedded water flows into the Middle East in the form of grain than flows in the Nile.

In addition, there are significant problems around the hegemonic doctrine of the water crisis. Many authors point to relatively low water provision per capita by states and suggest that this will increase the likelihood of a state engaging in war with a neighbouring state, to obtain the water necessary for its population. This is normally a conceptual leap that produces

1. That is, according to Thomas Malthus (1766–1834), a scholar who predicted population growth would put a strain on natural resources, among other things.

the incorrect corollary of conflict, but is also frequently a problem of data weaknesses around the per capita requirements. For instance, [economics student Philippe] Stucki cites the case of the Palestinians being under the worst water stress, with a per capita provision being in the region of 165m^3/year. Unfortunately, such an analysis is based on false actual provision data in this region. Based on the author's work on water provision in Lebanese Palestinian refugee camps, the actual provision is over 90m^3/month. Such a figure is highly likely to be representative of other camps in the region. If this example is representative of trends to exaggerate water pressures in the region, then we should be sceptical about claims of increasing water stress.

Furthermore, given that many water systems have a pipe leakage rate of fifty per cent, combined with a seventy per cent loss of agricultural water, significant efficiency enhancements could be made to existing infrastructure. Combined with desalination options in many water shortage–prone states, there is an overall capacity for technological and market-driven solutions to water scarcity.

Only a Failure of Politics Could Result in a Water War

Second, water wars are not caused by water, but rather an inability of politics. [University of Melbourne research fellow Jon] Barnett makes the case clear by arguing that water war would be a 'failure of politics' rather than the outcome of justified demands for essential resources. In this way, it is not scarcity that is the driver in the Malthusian sense, but a political, and politicised issue. This is most noticeable where conflict occurs in areas where there are both political tensions and water resources challenges. For example, there are absurd and exaggerated claims of a linkage between Israel's water management and surrounding states. In reality, conflict in this region is strongly influenced by political circumstance that speaks to a wider discourse around Israel's position in the Near East. That environmental constraints and pressures are woven into wider discourses of politics is no indication that they are the cause of conflict, but rather more that they are an important contextual factor that may be mobilised for political reasons. For instance, in 2000 Lebanon started building a small pumping station on the Wazzani river which is used by downstream Israel. This rapidly became a media issue in Israel, probably due to the heightened security discourse surrounding water. Claims were made that the action was comparable to the 1964 diversion of the Hasbani, an Arab coalition move to harm the Israeli economy. However, the story diminished even faster than it emerged, when officials on both sides showed their dismay at the emerging media frenzy. There are two key trends to note from this example: *first*, that wider discussions around water wars influence the articulation of war in reality, and *second*, the water component of the conflict is not significant, rather it acts as a trigger for the utilisation of wider political narratives. In essence, water is merely a tool for political ends.

States Gain More by Cooperating over Water Issues

Third, war over water is illogical. States are not inherently belligerent, but act in self-interested, utility-maximising ways. Rather, they engage in conflict if they stand to gain more than they lose. In the case of water, the costs of military engagement far outweigh the costs of cooperative engagement. For instance, [codirector of the Israel Palestine Center for Research and Information Gershon] Baskin points out that it would cost more for Israel to engage in war for the water resources of the West Bank than it would to buy the equivalent of the West Bank's aquifers from elsewhere.

Water war protagonists also present the weak argument that there is a unique situation in the Middle East of the possibility of state territories changing, with water-related land grabs. [As US diplomat Charles Maynes has argued] 'Victory may bring land that offers more resources—either water or oil.' This is not the case. State territories have been extremely stable for over a hundred years—conflict that attempts to enlarge boundaries would problematise the very existence and legitimacy of the state itself. By contrast, if they stand to gain by establishing cooperative relationships with other states in the international system, they will. It is difficult to see how good water management, which frequently demands cooperation, can be conducted through the use of conflict.

That said, there *are* incidences of water-related conflict on the intrastate level. For instance, in summer 2000, clashes involving thousands of farmers and police occurred in the Huang He river basin [in] China over government policy changes that meant a local dam runoff would no longer supply irrigation water for farmers but instead be used for urbanisation. In addition, in Pakistan there have been clashes between farmers in Punjab and Sindh province over control of the Indus. But these are not resource pressure issues—rather water acts as one of many other triggers in a wider problem of social injustice and political discourses.

The Water Cooperation Thesis

Given these conceptual and practical limitations, the link between water and war is at best contextual. However, water has an important role to play as a nexus of cooperation between states. As such the cooperative approach is overwhelmingly the most frequent response to water challenges between states. [In a 2009 issue of *Nature*, Wendy] Barnaby points out that 'Cooperation [. . .] is the dominant response to a shared water resource.'

Indeed, of the 263 international waterways in the world, all are managed more or less peacefully. This is supported by a substantial body of legislative and trans-boundary institution building—for instance between 805 and 1984, global states signed over 3,600 water-related treaties. Equally, of thirty-five cases of trans-boundary freshwater management, the most effective management strategy has universally been that of good relations.

Indeed, a cooperative international sphere, in which non-escalatory options are privileged, is likely to go hand in hand with a more peaceful internal state. Additionally according to some, cooperation on the water issue could act as a nucleus for further cooperative acts in other spheres, triggering linkages between states at a multiplicity of levels and opening communication channels normally severed by conflict. This has considerable conceptual purchase as has been welcomed as a potential in policy circles, particularly as it fits well with a political agenda of inclusivity. As such, there has been a growth of alternative water management strategies that incorporate the crucial local and regional levels in addition to the state level of analysis, attempting to address wider social ills while at the same time meeting water needs. While 'paradigm shift' may be a slightly premature analysis there is certainly a change in attitudes towards inclusivity. And while water acting as a social and political panacea in the 'developing' world is unlikely, the potential for cooperation needs continued and sustained exploration.

"*In 2012 and beyond, energy and conflict will be bound ever more tightly together, lending increasing importance to the key geographical flash points in our resource-constrained world.*"

Disputes over Energy Supplies May Be the Cause of Future Wars

Michael T. Klare

In the following viewpoint, Michael T. Klare contends that in a world facing energy shortages, disputes over energy-rich regions will become more prevalent and may lead to conflict. Klare identifies three areas—the Strait of Hormuz, the South China Sea, and the Caspian Sea basin—that may become focal points of international clashes over oil and natural gas. Klare insists that these regions are already experiencing political and ethnic tensions, making them powder kegs if sparks fly over energy disagreements. Klare is also careful to note that these are only some of the energy-rich areas of the globe that could erupt into violence if nations begin to quarrel about accessing or controlling energy resources. Michael T. Klare is a professor of peace and world security studies at Hampshire College in Amherst, Massachusetts. His latest book, The Race for What's Left: The Global Scramble for the World's Last Resources, *addresses the topic of looming energy wars.*

As you read, consider the following questions:

1. What are SLOCs, as Klare defines them?

2. According to the author, what country has threatened to stop oil flowing through the Strait of Hormuz if the United States imposes sanctions on that country's oil exports?

3. As Klare reports, about how much oil and natural gas is contained in the Caspian Sea region?

Welcome to an edgy world where a single incident at an energy "choke point" could set a region aflame, provoking bloody encounters, boosting oil prices, and putting the global economy at risk. With energy demand on the rise and sources of supply dwindling, we are, in fact, entering a new epoch—the Geo-Energy Era—in which disputes over vital resources will dominate world affairs. In 2012 and beyond, energy and conflict will be bound ever more tightly together, lending increasing importance to the key geographical flash points in our resource-constrained world.

The Pivotal Landmarks of the Geo-Energy Era

Take the Strait of Hormuz, already making headlines and shaking energy markets as 2012 begins. Connecting the Persian Gulf and the Indian Ocean, it lacks imposing geographical features like the Rock of Gibraltar or the Golden Gate Bridge. In an energy-conscious world, however, it may possess greater strategic significance than any passageway on the planet. Every day, according to the U.S. Department of Energy, tankers carrying some 17 million barrels of oil—representing 20% of the world's daily supply—pass through this vital artery.

So last month [in December 2011], when a senior Iranian official threatened to block the strait in response to Washington's tough new economic sanctions, oil prices instantly soared. While the U.S. military has vowed to keep the strait open, doubts about the safety of future oil shipments and worries about a potentially unending, nerve-jangling crisis involving Washington, Tehran [Iran], and Tel Aviv [Israel] have energy experts predicting high oil prices for months to come, meaning further woes for a slowing global economy.

The Strait of Hormuz is, however, only one of several hot spots where energy, politics, and geography are likely to mix in dangerous ways in 2012 and beyond. Keep your eye as well on the East and South China Seas, the Caspian Sea basin, and an energy-rich Arctic that is losing its sea ice. In all of these places, countries are disputing control over the production and transportation of energy, and arguing about national boundaries and/or rights of passage.

In the years to come, the location of energy supplies and of energy supply routes—pipelines, oil ports, and tanker routes—will be pivotal landmarks on the global strategic map. Key producing areas, like the Persian Gulf, will remain critically important, but so will oil choke points like the Strait of Hormuz and the Strait of Malacca (between the Indian Ocean and the South China Sea) and the "sea lines of communication," or SLOCs (as naval strategists like to call them), connecting producing areas to overseas markets. More and more, the major powers led by the United States, Russia, and China will restructure their militaries to fight in such locales.

You can already see this in the elaborate defense strategic guidance document, "Sustaining U.S. Global Leadership," unveiled at the Pentagon on January 5th [2012] by President [Barack] Obama and Secretary of Defense Leon Panetta. While envisioning a smaller Army and Marine Corps, it calls for increased emphasis on air and naval capabilities, especially those geared to the protection or control of international energy and trade networks. Though it tepidly reaffirmed historic American ties to Europe and the Middle East, overwhelming emphasis was placed on bolstering U.S. power in "the arc extending from the Western Pacific and East Asia into the Indian Ocean and South Asia."

In the new Geo-Energy Era, the control of energy and of its transport to market will lie at the heart of recurring global crises. This year, keep your eyes on three energy hot spots in particular: the Strait of Hormuz, the South China Sea, and the Caspian Sea basin.

The Strait of Hormuz: Oil Artery

A narrow stretch of water separating Iran from Oman and the United Arab Emirates (UAE), the strait is the sole maritime link between the oil-rich Persian Gulf region and the rest of the world. A striking percentage of the oil produced by Iran, Iraq, Kuwait, Qatar, Saudi Arabia, and the UAE is carried by tanker through this passageway on a daily basis, making it (in the words of the Department of Energy) "the world's most important oil choke point." Some analysts believe that any sustained blockage in the strait could trigger a 50% increase in the price of oil and trigger a full-scale global recession or depression.

American leaders have long viewed the strait as a strategic fixture in their global plans that must be defended at any cost. It was an outlook first voiced by President Jimmy Carter in January 1980, on the heels of the Soviet invasion and occupation of Afghanistan which had, he told Congress, "brought Soviet military forces to within 300 miles of the Indian Ocean and close to the Strait of Hormuz, a waterway through which most of the world's oil must flow." The American response, he insisted, must be unequivocal: Any attempt by a hostile power to block the waterway would henceforth be viewed as "an assault on the vital interests of the United States of America," and "repelled by any means necessary, including military force."

Much has changed in the Gulf region since Carter issued his famous decree, known since as the Carter Doctrine, and established the U.S. Central Command (CENTCOM) to guard the strait—but not Washington's determination to ensure the unhindered flow of oil there. Indeed, President Obama has made it clear that, even if CENTCOM ground forces were to leave Afghanistan, as they have Iraq, there would be no reduction in the command's air and naval presence in the greater Gulf area.

It is conceivable that the Iranians will put Washington's capabilities to the test. On December 27th [2011], Iran's first vice president Mohammad-Reza Rahimi said, "If [the Americans] impose sanctions on Iran's oil exports, then even one drop of oil cannot flow from the Strait of Hormuz." Similar statements have since been made by other senior officials (and contradicted as well by yet others). In addition, the Iranians recently conducted elaborate naval exercises in the Arabian Sea near the eastern mouth of the strait, and more such maneuvers are said to be forthcoming. At the same time, the commanding general of Iran's army suggested that the USS *John C. Stennis*, an American aircraft carrier just leaving the Gulf, should not return. "The Islamic Republic of Iran," he added ominously, "will not repeat its warning."

Might the Iranians actually block the strait? Many analysts believe that the statements by Rahimi and his colleagues are bluster and bluff meant to rattle Western leaders, send oil prices higher, and win future concessions if negotiations ever recommence over their country's nuclear program. Economic conditions in Iran are, however, becoming more desperate, and it is always possible that the country's hard-pressed, hard-line leaders may feel the urge to take some dramatic action, even if it invites a powerful U.S. counterstrike. Whatever the case, the Strait of Hormuz will remain a focus of international attention in 2012, with global oil prices closely following the rise and fall of tensions there.

The South China Sea: Tensions over Untapped Energy Reserves

The South China Sea is a semi-enclosed portion of the western Pacific bounded by China to the north, Vietnam to the west, the Philippines to the east, and the island of Borneo (shared by Brunei, Indonesia, and Malaysia) to the south. The sea also incorporates two largely uninhabited island chains, the Paracels and the Spratlys. Long an important fishing ground, it has also been a major avenue for commercial shipping between East Asia and Europe, the Middle East, and Africa. More recently, it acquired significance as a potential source of oil and natural gas, large reserves of which are now believed to lie in subsea areas surrounding the Paracels and Spratlys.

With the discovery of oil and gas deposits, the South China Sea has been transformed into a cockpit of international friction. At least some islands in this energy-rich area are claimed by every one of the surrounding countries, including China— which claims them all, and has demonstrated a willingness to use military force to assert dominance in the region. Not surprisingly, this has put it in conflict with the other claimants, including several with close military ties to the United States. As a result, what started out as a regional matter, involving China and various members of the Association of Southeast Asian Nations (ASEAN), has become a prospective tussle between the world's two leading powers.

To press their claims, Brunei, Malaysia, Vietnam, and the Philippines have all sought to work collectively through ASEAN, believing a multilateral approach will give them greater negotiating clout than one-on-one dealings with China.

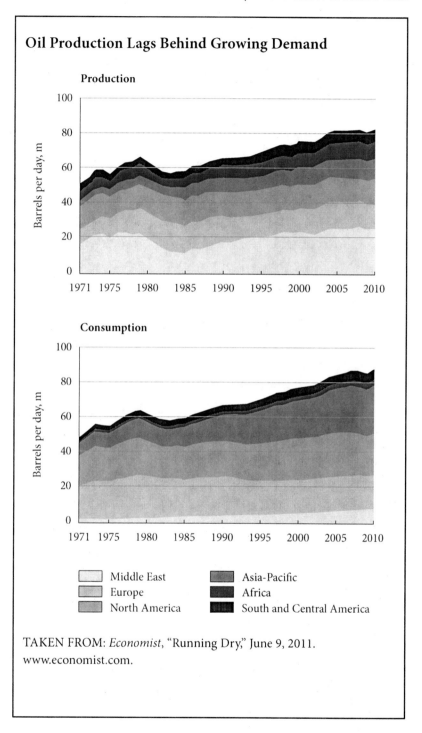

Oil Production Lags Behind Growing Demand

TAKEN FROM: *Economist*, "Running Dry," June 9, 2011.
www.economist.com.

For their part, the Chinese have insisted that all disputes must be resolved bilaterally, a situation in which they can more easily bring their economic and military power to bear. Previously preoccupied with Iraq and Afghanistan, the United States has now entered the fray, offering full-throated support to the ASEAN countries in their efforts to negotiate en masse with Beijing.

Chinese Foreign Minister Yang Jiechi promptly warned the United States not to interfere. Any such move "will only make matters worse and the resolution more difficult," he declared. The result was an instant war of words between Beijing and Washington. During a visit to the Chinese capital in July 2011, Chairman of the Joint Chiefs of Staff Admiral Mike Mullen delivered a barely concealed threat when it came to possible future military action. "The worry, among others that I have," he commented, "is that the ongoing incidents could spark a miscalculation, and an outbreak that no one anticipated." To drive the point home, the United States has conducted a series of conspicuous military exercises in the South China Sea, including some joint maneuvers with ships from Vietnam and the Philippines. Not to be outdone, China responded with naval maneuvers of its own. It's a perfect formula for future "incidents" at sea.

The South China Sea has long been on the radar screens of those who follow Asian affairs, but it only attracted global attention when, in November, President Obama traveled to Australia and announced, with remarkable bluntness, a new U.S. strategy aimed at confronting Chinese power in Asia and the Pacific. "As we plan and budget for the future," he told members of the Australian Parliament in Canberra, "we will allocate the resources necessary to maintain our strong military presence in this region." A key feature of this effort would be to ensure "maritime security" in the South China Sea.

While in Australia, President Obama also announced the establishment of a new U.S. base at Darwin on that country's northern coast, as well as expanded military ties with Indonesia and the Philippines. In January, the president similarly placed special emphasis on projecting U.S. power in the region when he went to the Pentagon to discuss changes in the American military posture in the world.

Beijing will undoubtedly take its own set of steps, no less belligerent, to protect its growing interests in the South China Sea. Where this will lead remains, of course, unknown. After the Strait of Hormuz, however, the South China Sea may be the global energy choke point where small mistakes or provocations could lead to bigger confrontations in 2012 and beyond.

The Caspian Sea Basin: Contested Borders and Ethnic Tensions

The Caspian Sea is an inland body of water bordered by Russia, Iran, and three former republics of the USSR [Union of Soviet Socialist Republics, or Russia]: Azerbaijan, Kazakhstan, and Turkmenistan. In the immediate area as well are the former Soviet lands of Armenia, Georgia, Kyrgyzstan, and Tajikistan. All of these old SSRs [Soviet Socialist Republics] are, to one degree or another, attempting to assert their autonomy from Moscow and establish independent ties with the United States, the European Union, Iran, Turkey, and, increasingly, China. All are wracked by internal schisms and/or involved in border disputes with their neighbors. The region would be a hotbed of potential conflict even if the Caspian basin did not harbor some of the world's largest undeveloped reserves of oil and natural gas, which could easily bring it to a boil.

This is not the first time that the Caspian has been viewed as a major source of oil, and so potential conflict. In the late nineteenth century, the region around the city of Baku—then part of the Russian empire, now in Azerbaijan—was a prolific source of petroleum and so a major strategic prize. Future Soviet dictator Joseph Stalin first gained notoriety there as a leader of militant oil workers, and [Adolf] Hitler sought to capture it during his ill-fated 1941 invasion of the USSR. After World War II, however, the region lost its importance as an oil producer when Baku's onshore fields dried up. Now, fresh discoveries are being made in offshore areas of the Caspian itself and in previously undeveloped areas of Kazakhstan and Turkmenistan.

According to energy giant BP, the Caspian area harbors as much as 48 billion barrels of oil (mostly buried in Azerbaijan and Kazakhstan) and 449 trillion cubic feet of natural gas (with the largest supply in Turkmenistan). This puts the region ahead of North and South America in total gas reserves and Asia in oil reserves. But producing all this energy and delivering it to foreign markets will be a monumental task. The region's energy infrastructure is woefully inadequate and the Caspian itself provides no maritime outlet to other seas, so all that oil and gas must travel by pipeline or rail.

Russia, long the dominant power in the region, is pursuing control over the transportation routes by which Caspian oil and gas will reach markets. It is upgrading Soviet-era pipelines that link the former SSRs to Russia or building new ones and, to achieve a near monopoly over the marketing of all this energy, bringing traditional diplomacy, strong-arm tactics, and outright bribery to bear on regional leaders (many of whom once served in the Soviet bureaucracy) to ship their energy via Russia. As recounted in my book *Rising Powers, Shrinking Planet*, Washington sought to thwart these efforts by sponsoring the construction of alternative pipelines that avoid Russian territory, crossing Azerbaijan, Georgia, and Turkey to the Mediterranean (notably the BTC, or Baku-Tbilisi-Ceyhan pipeline), while Beijing is building its own pipelines linking the Caspian area to western China.

All of these pipelines cross through areas of ethnic unrest and pass near various contested regions like rebellious Chechnya and breakaway South Ossetia. As a result, both China and the U.S. have wedded their pipeline operations to military assistance for countries along the routes. Fearful of an American presence, military or otherwise, in the former territories of the Soviet Union, Russia has responded with military moves of its own, including its brief August 2008 war with Georgia, which took place along the BTC route.

Given the magnitude of the Caspian's oil and gas reserves, many energy firms are planning new production operations in the region, along with the pipelines needed to bring the oil and gas to market. The European Union, for example, hopes to build a new natural gas pipeline called Nabucco from Azerbaijan through Turkey to Austria. Russia has proposed a competing conduit called South Stream. All of these efforts involve the geopolitical interests of major powers, ensuring that the Caspian region will remain a potential source of international crisis and conflict.

Potential Sparks and Flash Points

In the new Geo-Energy Era, the Strait of Hormuz, the South China Sea, and the Caspian basin hardly stand alone as potential energy flash points. The East China Sea, where China and Japan are contending for a contested undersea natural gas field, is another, as are the waters surrounding the Falkland Islands, where both Britain and Argentina hold claims to undersea oil reserves, as will be the globally warming Arctic whose resources are claimed by many countries. One thing is certain: Wherever the sparks may fly, there's oil in the water and danger at hand in 2012.

> *"In a world of increasing interdependence, energy security will depend much on how countries manage their relations with one another."*

Energy Interdependence Encourages Nations to Work Together and Avoid Serious Energy Disruptions

Daniel Yergin

Daniel Yergin is an economics author and the cofounder and chairman of Cambridge Energy Research Associates, an energy research consultancy firm. His most well-known works are The Prize: The Epic Quest for Oil, Money and Power *and* The Quest: Energy, Security, and the Remaking of the Modern World. *In the following viewpoint, Yergin asserts that energy security must be a global, not national, concern. The shocks caused by disruptions in energy flow—whether from terrorists, conflicts, or natural disasters—can be mitigated, Yergin argues, by diversifying the mix of energy resources available to each nation and by working collectively to secure supplies, energy pathways, and*

Daniel Yergin, "Ensuring Energy Security," *Foreign Affairs*, v. 85, no. 2, March/April 2006. Reprinted by permission of FOREIGN AFFAIRS. Copyright 2006 by the Council on Foreign Relations Inc. www.ForeignAffairs.com.

markets. Yergin believes that while threats to energy security will arise from time to time, the world can take precautions to avoid serious consequences.

As you read, consider the following questions:

1. As Yergin states, the dispute between Russia and what other country temporarily cut natural gas supplies to Europe?

2. How many barrels of oil are consumed every day throughout the world, according to Yergin?

3. In the viewpoint, how much money does the IEA estimate nations will have to invest in energy development over the next twenty-five years?

Energy security will be the number one topic on the agenda when the group of eight highly industrialized countries (G8) meets in St. Petersburg in July [2006]. The renewed focus on energy security is driven in part by an exceedingly tight oil market and by high oil prices, which have doubled over the past three years. But it is also fueled by the threat of terrorism, instability in some exporting nations, a nationalist backlash, fears of a scramble for supplies, geopolitical rivalries, and countries' fundamental need for energy to power their economic growth.

In the background—but not too far back—is renewed anxiety over whether there will be sufficient resources to meet the world's energy requirements in the decades ahead.

Concerns over energy security are not limited to oil. Power blackouts on both the East and West Coasts of the United States, in Europe, and in Russia, as well as chronic shortages of electric power in China, India, and other developing countries, have raised worries about the reliability of electricity supply systems. When it comes to natural gas, rising demand and constrained supplies mean that North America can no longer be self-reliant, and so the United States is joining the new global market in natural gas that will link countries, continents, and prices together in an unprecedented way.

Energy Vulnerability

At the same time, a new range of vulnerabilities has become more evident. [The terrorist group] al-Qaeda has threatened to attack what [its leader] Osama bin Laden calls the "hinges" of the world's economy, that is, its critical infrastructure of which energy is among the most crucial elements. The world will increasingly depend on new sources of supply from places where security systems are still being developed, such as the oil and natural gas fields offshore of West Africa and in the Caspian Sea. And the vulnerabilities are not limited to threats of terrorism, political turmoil, armed conflict, and piracy. In August and September 2005, Hurricanes Katrina and Rita delivered the world's first integrated energy shock, simultaneously disrupting flows of oil, natural gas, and electric power.

Events since the beginning of this year [2006] have underlined the significance of the issue. The Russian-Ukrainian natural gas dispute temporarily cut supplies to Europe. Rising tensions over Tehran's nuclear program brought threats from Iran, the second-largest OPEC [Organization of the Petroleum Exporting Countries] producer, to "unleash an oil crisis." And scattered attacks on some oil facilities reduced exports from Nigeria, which is a major supplier to the United States.

Since [World War I], the key to energy security has been diversification. This remains true, but a wider approach is now required that takes into account the rapid evolution of the global energy trade, supply-chain vulnerabilities, terrorism, and the integration of major new economies into the world market.

Differing Ideas of Energy Security

Although in the developed world the usual definition of energy security is simply the availability of sufficient supplies at affordable prices, different countries interpret what the concept means for them differently. Energy-exporting countries focus on maintaining the "security of demand" for their exports, which after all generate the overwhelming share of their government revenues. For Russia, the aim is to reassert state control over "strategic resources" and gain primacy over the main pipelines and market channels through which it ships its hydrocarbons to international markets. The concern for developing countries is how changes in energy prices affect their balance of payments. For China and India, energy security now lies in their ability to rapidly adjust to their new dependence on global markets, which represents a major shift away from their former commitments to self-sufficiency. For Japan, it means offsetting its stark scarcity of domestic resources through diversification, trade, and investment. In Europe, the major debate centers on how to manage dependence on imported natural gas—and in most countries, aside from France and Finland, whether to build new nuclear power plants and perhaps to return to (clean) coal. And the United States must face the uncomfortable fact that its goal of "energy independence"—a phrase that has become a mantra since it was first articulated by Richard Nixon four weeks after the 1973 [oil] embargo was put in place—is increasingly at odds with reality. . . .

The current energy security system was created in response to the 1973 Arab oil embargo to ensure coordination among the industrialized countries in the event of a disruption in supply, encourage collaboration on energy policies, avoid bruising scrambles for supplies, and deter any future use of an "oil weapon" by exporters. Its key elements are the Paris-based International Energy Agency (IEA), whose members are the industrialized countries; strategic stockpiles of oil, including the U.S. Strategic Petroleum Reserve; continued monitoring and analysis of energy markets and policies; and energy conservation and coordinated emergency sharing of supplies in the event of a disruption. The emergency system was set up to offset major disruptions that threatened the global economy and stability, not to manage prices and the commodity cycle. Since the system's inception in the 1970s, a coordinated emergency drawdown of strategic stockpiles has occurred only twice: on the eve of the Gulf War in 1991 and in the autumn of 2005 after Hurricane Katrina. (The system was also readied in anticipation of possible use before January 1, 2000, because of concerns over the potential problems arising from the Y2K computer bug, during the shutdown of production in Venezuela in 2002–3, and in the spring of 2003, before the [US-led] invasion of Iraq.)

Principles of Energy Security

Experience has shown that to maintain energy security, countries must abide by several principles. The first and most familiar is what [First Lord of the Admiralty Winston] Churchill urged more than 90 years ago: diversification of supply. Multiplying one's supply sources reduces the impact of a disruption in supply from one source by providing alternatives, serving the interests of both consumers and producers, for whom stable markets are a prime concern. But diversification is not enough. A second principle is resilience, a "security margin" in the energy supply system that provides a buffer against shocks and facilitates recovery after disruptions. Resilience can come from many factors, including sufficient spare production capacity, strategic reserves, backup supplies of equipment, adequate storage capacity along the supply chain, and the stockpiling of critical parts for electric power production and distribution, as well as carefully conceived plans for responding to disruptions that may affect large regions. Hence the third principle: recognizing the reality of integration. There is only one oil market, a complex and worldwide system that moves and consumes about 86 million barrels of oil every day. For all consumers, security resides in the stability of this market. Secession is not an option.

A fourth principle is the importance of information. High-quality information underpins well-functioning markets. On an international level, the IEA has led the way in improving the flow of information about world markets and energy prospects. That work is being complemented by the new International Energy Forum, which will seek to integrate information from producers and consumers. Information is no less crucial in a crisis, when consumer panics can be instigated by a mixture of actual disruptions, rumors, and fear. Reality can be obscured by accusations, acrimony, outrage, and a fevered hunt for conspiracies, transforming a difficult situation into something much worse. In such situations, governments and the private sector should collaborate to counter panics with high-quality, timely information. The U.S. government can promote flexibility and market adjustments by expediting its communication with companies and permitting the exchange of information among them, with appropriate antitrust safeguards, when necessary.

The Globalization of the Energy Supply Chain

As important as these principles are, the past several years have highlighted the need to expand the concept of energy security in two critical dimensions: the recognition of the globalization of the energy security system, which can be achieved especially by engaging China and India, and the acknowledgment of the fact that the entire energy supply chain needs to be protected.

China's thirst for energy has become a decisive plot element in suspense novels and films. Even in the real world there is no shortage of suspicion: Some in the United States see a Chinese grand strategy to preempt the United States and the West when it comes to new oil and gas supplies, and some strategists in Beijing fear that the United States may someday try to interdict China's foreign energy supplies. But the actual situation is less dramatic. Despite all the attention being paid to China's efforts to secure international petroleum reserves, for example, the entire amount that China currently produces per day outside of its own borders is equivalent to just 10 percent of the daily production of one of the super-major oil companies. If there were a serious controversy between the United States and China involving oil or gas, it would likely arise not because of a competition for the resources themselves, but rather because they had become part of larger foreign policy issues (such as a clash over a specific regime or over how to respond to Iran's nuclear program). Indeed, from the viewpoint of consumers in North America, Europe, and Japan, Chinese and Indian investment in the development of new energy supplies around the world is not a threat but something to be desired, because it means there will be more energy available for everyone in the years ahead as India's and China's demand grows.

It would be wiser—and indeed it is urgent—to engage these two giants in the global network of trade and investment rather than see them tilt toward a mercantilist, state-to-state approach. Engaging India and China will require understanding what energy security means for them. Both countries are rapidly moving from self-sufficiency to integration into the world economy, which means they will grow increasingly dependent on global markets even as they are under tremendous pressure to deliver economic growth for their huge populations, which cope with energy shortages and blackouts on a daily basis. Thus, the primary concern for both China and India is to ensure that they have sufficient energy to support economic growth and prevent debilitating energy shortfalls that could trigger social and political turbulence. For India, where the balance-of-payments crisis of 1990 is still on policy makers' minds, international production is also a way to hedge against high oil prices. And so India and China, amid other key countries such as Brazil, should be brought into coordina-

Tools That Have Helped Weather Interruptions in Oil Supply

While global dependence on oil imports has generally increased since 1980, vulnerability to short-term interruptions has not. The world has weathered several major interruptions since 1980, namely the tanker war [between Iran and Iraq] in the late 80s, the [Iraqi] invasion of Kuwait in 1990, and the [US-led] invasion of Iraq in 2003, none of which has produced economic damage approaching either the magnitude or the duration of the 70s disruptions. In part, this is attributable to measures adopted to manage such risks, including building strategic reserves, promoting free trade and investment, and developing traditional diplomatic and military instruments to secure that trade.

American Petroleum Institute,
"Achieving Energy Security in an Interdependent World," 2013.
www.api.org.

tion with the existing IEA energy security system to assure them that their interests will be protected in the event of turbulence and to ensure that the system works more effectively.

Protecting Energy Systems and Markets

The current model of energy security, which was born of the 1973 crisis, focuses primarily on how to handle any disruption of oil supplies from producing countries. Today, the concept of energy security needs to be expanded to include the protection of the entire energy supply chain and infrastructure—an awesome task. In the United States alone, there are more than 150 refineries, 4,000 offshore platforms, 160,000 miles of oil pipelines, facilities to handle 15 million barrels of oil a day of imports and exports, 10,400 power plants, 160,000 miles of high-voltage electric power transmission lines and millions of miles of electric power distribution wires, 410 underground gas storage fields, and 1.4 million miles of natural gas pipelines. None of the world's complex, integrated supply chains were built with security, defined in this broad way, in mind. Hurricanes Katrina and Rita brought a new perspective to the security question by demonstrating how fundamental the electric grid is to everything else. After the storms, the Gulf Coast refineries and the big U.S. pipelines were unable to operate—not because they were damaged, but because they could not get power.

Energy interdependence and the growing scale of energy trade require continuing collaboration among both producers and consumers to ensure the security of the entire supply chain. Long-distance, cross-border pipelines are becoming an ever-larger fixture in the global energy trade. There are also many choke points along the transportation routes of seaborne oil and, in many cases, liquefied natural gas (LNG) that create particular vulnerabilities: the Strait of Hormuz, which lies at the entrance to the Persian Gulf; the Suez Canal, which connects the Red Sea and the Mediterranean; the Bab-el-Mandeb strait, which provides entrance to the Red Sea; the Bosporus Strait, which is a major export channel for Russian and Caspian oil; and the Strait of Malacca, through which passes 80 percent of Japan's and South Korea's oil and about half of China's. Ships commandeered and scuttled in these strategic waterways could disrupt supply lines for extended periods. Securing pipelines and choke points will require augmented monitoring as well as the development of multilateral rapid-response capabilities. . . .

Markets need to be recognized as a source of security in themselves. The energy security system was created when energy prices were regulated in the United States, energy trading was only just beginning, and futures markets were several years away. Today, large, flexible, and well-functioning energy markets provide security by absorbing shocks and allowing supply and demand to respond more quickly and with greater ingenuity than a controlled system could. Such markets will guarantee security for the growing LNG market and thereby boost the confidence of the countries that import it. Thus, governments must resist the temptation to bow to political pressure and micromanage markets. Intervention and controls, however well meaning, can backfire, slowing and even preventing the movement of supplies to respond to disruptions. At least in the United States, any price spike or disruption evokes the memory of the infamous gas lines of the 1970s—even for those who were only toddlers then (and perhaps even for those not yet born at the time). Yet those lines were to a considerable degree self-inflicted—the consequence of price controls and a heavy-handed allocation system that sent gasoline where it was not needed and denied its being sent where it was. . . .

The U.S. government and the private sector should also make a renewed commitment to energy efficiency and conservation. Although often underrated, the impact of conservation on the economy has been enormous over the past several decades. Over the past 30 years, U.S. GDP [gross domestic product] has grown by 150 percent, while U.S. energy consumption has grown by only 25 percent. In the 1970s and 1980s, many considered that kind of decoupling impossible, or at least certain to be economically ruinous. True, many of the gains in energy efficiency have come because the U.S. economy is "lighter," as former Federal Reserve chair Alan Greenspan has put it, than it was three decades ago—that is, GDP today is composed of less manufacturing and more services (especially information technology) than could have been imagined in the 1970s. But the basic point remains: Conservation has worked. Current and future advances in technology could permit very large additional gains, which would be highly beneficial not only for advanced economies such as that of the United States, but also for the economies of countries such as India and China (in fact, China has recently made conservation a priority).

Finally, the investment climate itself must become a key concern in energy security. There needs to be a continual flow of investment and technology in order for new resources to be developed. The IEA recently estimated that as much as $17 trillion will be required for new energy development over the next 25 years. These capital flows will not materialize without reasonable and stable investment frameworks, timely decision making by governments, and open markets. How to facilitate energy investment will be one of the critical questions on the G8's energy security agenda in 2006.

Easing Future Energy Shocks

Inevitably, there will be shocks to energy markets in the future. Some of the possible causes may be roughly foreseeable, such as coordinated attacks by terrorists, disruptions in the Middle East and Africa, or turmoil in Latin America that affects output in Venezuela, the third-largest OPEC producer. Other possible causes, however, may come as a surprise. The offshore oil industry has long built facilities to withstand a "hundred-year storm"—but nobody anticipated that two such devastating storms would strike the energy complex in the Gulf of Mexico within a matter of weeks. And the creators of the IEA emergency sharing system in the 1970s never for a moment considered that it might have to be activated to blunt the effects of a disruption in the United States.

Diversification will remain the fundamental starting principle of energy security for both oil and gas. Today, however, it will likely also require developing a new generation of nuclear power and "clean coal" technologies and encouraging a growing role for a variety of renewable energy sources as they become more competitive. It will also require investing in new technologies, ranging from near-term ones, such as the conversion of natural gas into a liquid fuel, to ones that are still in the lab, such as the biological engineering of energy supplies. Investment in technology all along the energy spectrum is surging today, and this will have a positive effect not only on the future energy picture but also on the environment.

Yet energy security also exists in a larger context. In a world of increasing interdependence, energy security will depend much on how countries manage their relations with one another, whether bilaterally or within multilateral frameworks. That is why energy security will be one of the main challenges for U.S. foreign policy in the years ahead. Part of that challenge will be anticipating and assessing the "what ifs." And that requires looking not only around the corner, but also beyond the ups and downs of cycles to both the reality of an ever more complex and integrated global energy system and the relations among the countries that participate in it.

"*Those killed in the name of religion have, in fact, been a tiny fraction in the bloody history of human conflict.*"

Most Wars Have Been Fought for Secular, Not Religious, Reasons

Alan Lurie

Alan Lurie refutes in the following viewpoint that religion is a primary cause of warfare. Although Lurie acknowledges that some wars have been fought in the name of religion, history shows that far more conflicts have arisen over greed, political power, and simple hatred. In fact, Lurie asserts that religions promote peace over warfare, relegating the latter as a last resort if peaceful overtures fail. Alan Lurie is an ordained rabbi and managing director at Grubb & Ellis, a national real estate service firm.

As you read, consider the following questions:

1. About what percentage of all wars in human history have involved a religious cause, according to Lurie?

2. How does Lurie characterize Israelite leader Joshua's conquest of Canaan and some other wars described in the Bible?

3. What is "the highest religious aspiration for which we must work," in Lurie's view?

There are many common misconceptions about religion that are often taken as unquestioned facts, such as the idea that religious people are inherently antiscience, that a literal reading of holy texts is the "true" religious stance, that faith is incompatible with reason, and that all religions claim to possess sole and absolute truth.

While all these ideas are true for a minority of the population, they do not describe normative religious beliefs and practices for the majority of believers. It is understandable that these misconceptions persist, though, because they come from the loudest voices on the extremes, and like other polarizing positions in politics and culture are simplistic ideas that promote easy "us vs. them" thinking. But there is one common misconception about religion that is voiced often and consistently as an obvious truth—often by educated, thoughtful people—that is just not factually true: the idea that religion has been the cause of most wars.

An Objective Look at History

In his hilarious analysis of the 10 Commandments, George Carlin said to loud applause, "More people have been killed in the name of God than for any other reason," and many take this idea as an historical fact. When I hear someone state that religion has caused most wars, though, I will often ask the person to name these wars. The response is typically, "Come on! The Crusades, the Inquisition, Northern Ireland, the Middle East, 9/11. Need I name more?"

Well, yes, we do need to name more, because while clearly there were wars that had religion as the prime cause, an objective look at history reveals that those killed in the name of religion have, in fact, been a tiny fraction in the bloody history of human conflict. In their recently published book, *En-*

cyclopedia of Wars, authors Charles Phillips and Alan Axelrod document the history of recorded warfare, and from their list of 1,763 wars only 123 have been classified to involve a religious cause, accounting for less than 7 percent of all wars and less than 2 percent of all people killed in warfare. While, for example, it is estimated that approximately one to three million people were tragically killed in the Crusades, and perhaps 3,000 in the Inquisition, nearly 35 million soldiers and civilians died in the senseless, and secular, slaughter of World War I alone.

History simply does not support the hypothesis that religion is the major cause of conflict. The wars of the ancient world were rarely, if ever, based on religion. These wars were for territorial conquest, to control borders, secure trade routes, or respond to an internal challenge to political authority. In fact, the ancient conquerors, whether Egyptian, Babylonian, Persian, Greek, or Roman, openly welcomed the religious beliefs of those they conquered, and often added the new gods to their own pantheon.

Medieval and Renaissance wars were also typically about control and wealth as city-states vied for power, often with the support, but rarely instigation, of the church. And the Mongol Asian rampage, which is thought to have killed nearly 30 million people, had no religious component whatsoever.

Most modern wars, including the Napoleonic campaign, the American Revolution, the French Revolution, the American Civil War, World War I, the Russia Revolution, World War II, and the conflicts in Korea and Vietnam, were not religious in nature or cause. While religious groups have been specifically targeted (most notably in World War II), to claim that religion was the cause is to blame the victim and to misunderstand the perpetrators' motives, which were nationalistic and ethnic, not religious.

Similarly, the vast numbers of genocides (those killed in ethnic cleanses, purges, etc., that are not connected to a de-

"Religious wars—and the real winner is. . ." cartoon by Wilfred Hildonen, www.Car toonStock.com.

clared war) are not based on religion. It's estimated that over 160 million civilians were killed in genocides in the 20th century alone, with nearly 100 million killed by the Communist states of the USSR [Union of Soviet Socialist Republics, or Soviet Union] and China. While some claim that communism itself is a "state religion"—because it has an absolute dictator whose word is law and a "holy book" of unchallenged rules—such a claim simply equates "religion" with the human desire for power, conformance, and control, making any distinctions with other human institutions meaningless.

Religion Teaches Peaceful Resolution to Conflict

Of course the Hebrew Bible chronicles many wars—most notably Moses' conflicts in the desert and Joshua's conquest of the nations of Canaan—and we may see these as examples of religiously sanctioned violence. Here, though, we must recognize that archeological evidence points to the conclusion that these conquests never occurred, or at least not as dramatically as described in the Bible. As one who reads the Bible for spiritual truths, not historical facts, I am, of course, quite happy that no such slaughters occurred. The ancient rabbis also understood these stories not as celebrated victories, but as warnings about the dangers of warfare.

Judaism has always taught that war may only be considered when there is a clear threat, and only after every other option has been exhausted. Avoiding war must be the goal. Deuteronomy states, "When you approach a city to do battle with it you should call to it in peace." In other words, even when threatened, seeking peace must be the first course of action. The ancient rabbis took this teaching so far as to flatly state, "In God's eyes the man stands high who makes peace between men. But he stands highest who establishes peace among the nations."

To be clear, this is not to say that religion is not a cause of conflict. Obviously it is, has been, and no doubt will continue to be. Clearly there are those who have committed horrendous acts based on religious zeal, and we must be alert to these threats and respond forcefully. But in a world with billions of people who are self-defined as religious, those who believe that violence is the will of God and that the murder of innocents is a holy act are a small, insane minority.

Peace is the highest religious aspiration for which we must work. As he envisioned a future where the world is perfected by the conscious acts of human beings, the ancient Hebrew prophet Isaiah wrote, "They shall beat their swords into ploughshares and their spears into pruning hooks: nation shall not lift up sword against nation, neither shall they learn war any more." While religions have often fallen well short of this utopian vision, we must recognize that greed, unbalanced power, and causeless hatred—not religion—are the causes of most wars, and eliminating these should be our focus.

Periodical Bibliography

The following articles have been selected to supplement the diverse views presented in this chapter.

Wendy Barnaby   "Do Nations Go to War over Water?," *Nature*, March 19, 2009.

Ed Blanche   "Middle East Water Wars," *Middle East*, June 2010.

William T. Cavanaugh   "The War on Terror: Secular or Sacred?," *Political Theology*, November 2011.

Ismael Hossein-Zadeh   "The Political Economy of US Wars of Choice: Are They Really Oil Wars?," *Perspectives on Global Development & Technology*, April 2009.

Roger Howard   "Peak Oil and Strategic Resource Wars," *Futurist*, September/October 2009.

Kerry Hutchinson   "Water Wars," *Middle East*, January/February 2012.

Toby Craig Jones   "America, Oil, and War in the Middle East," *Journal of American History*, June 2012.

Philippe Le Billion   "Oil Prices, Scarcity, and Geographies of War,"
and Alejandro   *Annals of the Association of American Geogra-*
Cervantes   *phers*, November 2009.

Heinrich Schäfer   "The Janus Face of Religion: On the Religious Factor in 'New Wars,'" *Numen*, 2004.

Chelsea Wald   "The Water's Edge," *New Scientist*, February 2012.

Fareed Zakaria   "The Radicals Are Desperate," *Newsweek*, March 15, 2004.

OPPOSING
VIEWPOINTS®
SERIES

CHAPTER 3

How Is America Faring in the War on Terror?

Chapter Preface

After the militant Islamic organization known as al Qaeda—an Arabic term meaning "the base"—hijacked airlines and crashed them into the World Trade Center and the Pentagon on September 11, 2001, also known as 9/11, America, with the support of Britain and other allies, spearheaded what was quickly dubbed the war on terror. Not a clearly defined international conflict with traditional military objectives, the war on terror is an ongoing fight against al Qaeda, its backers, and other perceived threats to national security in an effort to prevent another 9/11 catastrophe. Since its inception, the endeavor has grown to include surveillance of terrorists and presumed terrorist organizations, increased port and airport security, monitoring of potential nuclear proliferation, and even the waging of classical wars in Afghanistan (al Qaeda's initial base of operations) and Iraq (a nation assumed to be building weapons of mass destruction).

The Congressional Budget Office notes that the war has cost the United States $1.2 trillion over its first decade of operation, with some outside estimates doubling the price tag if related war spending not covered in the budget is included. Such a high price, coupled with a sense that policing and security measures will never end, has convinced many critics that the government's policy will keep the United States in a perpetual state of anxiety while draining national coffers. Writing in the November/December 2007 issue of *Foreign Affairs*, Philip H. Gordon pointedly asks, "Will this kind of war ever end? How long will it take? Would we see victory coming? Would we recognize it when it came?" To avoid continually asking such questions, some analysts suggest that with the successful US military raid in May 2011 that ended in the death of Osama bin Laden, the al Qaeda leader who claimed responsibility for the 9/11 attacks, and the progressive drawdown of troops in Iraq, the US government should declare victory in the war and refocus its efforts to other areas of foreign policy. The government, however, has made no such assertions. In fact, President Barack Obama—who inherited the war from his predecessor, George W. Bush—has kept much of the initial strategies in place, and while he extolled the military's ability to "get" bin Laden, he has otherwise refrained from perpetuating the notion that America is at war. His administration, for example, asked Pentagon speechwriters in 2009 to stop using the phrase "global war on terror" and opt for the less aggressive "overseas contingency operations." Whether such a move signals the president's desire for closure is unclear, but eleven years after 9/11, the war in Afghanistan continues and airport security check lines have become the norm.

Not everyone believes the death of Osama bin Laden heralds an allied victory in the war on terror. Charlie Szrom, an associate at the business consulting firm D.C. International Advisory, argues that though America should celebrate, the killing of bin Laden in a Pakistani compound suggests that America must strengthen its resolve to cut lifelines and financial backings that keep terrorists afloat. On the day after bin Laden's death, Szrom wrote in a post on the National Public Radio website, "Without friendly operating environments, terrorist groups will be unable to concoct plots, train operatives, and shelter leadership. . . . Bin Laden's death presents the U.S. with a real opportunity to shift the momentum on the ground back in our favor." On the same day, Brian Michael Jenkins warned on the *National Security Experts Blog* that despite the fact that al Qaeda is on the run, "it may morph to survive." He states that "developments on any of several fronts might even enable it to rise again." Thus, he concludes any claim of victory is likely premature and may even "complicate counterterrorist efforts."

In the chapter that follows, other experts offer their views on how America should pursue antiterrorist operations more than a decade after declaring war on al Qaeda.

> "We know the war on terror ... is a
> generational calling that requires the
> entire U.S. government and the inter-
> national community to act. . . . But
> there is no doubt in my mind that we
> will see victory in this struggle."

Winning the War on Terror: Marking Success and Confronting Challenges

Juan Zarate

Juan Zarate was deputy assistant to the president and deputy national security advisor for combating terrorism under George W. Bush when he argued in the following viewpoint that America and its allies are winning the war against terrorism. Zarate contends that in the years after the terrorist attacks of September 11, 2001, America has improved its defenses and made strategic partnerships to monitor and thwart terrorist activity. Zarate claims that al Qaeda—the group responsible for the September 11 tragedy—has been hunted and disrupted, and many Islamic leaders have condemned its violent tactics. Though he maintains the war on terror has not yet been won, Zarate believes victory is

Juan Zarate, "Winning the War on Terror: Marking Success and Confronting Challenges," Speech at Washington Institute Policy Forum, © 2008 The Washington Insitute for Near East Policy. Reprinted with permission.

assured. Juan Zarate is currently serving as senior advisor at the Center for Strategic and International Studies, a bipartisan think tank focusing on domestic and foreign policy.

As you read, consider the following questions:

1. As Zarate explains, how has the Bush government worked to undercut the image and ideology of al Qaeda around the globe?

2. What Arab tribe in Iraq has openly rejected al Qaeda's ideology, according to Zarate?

3. On the border of what two nations does Zarate claim al Qaeda has found safe haven?

On April 23, 2008, Juan Zarate, deputy national security advisor for combating terrorism, addressed a Washington Institute policy forum. The following are his prepared remarks.

Thank you to Rob Satloff, Michael Stein, and the Washington Institute for the kind invitation to speak today. It has been almost a year since I was here last to talk about the ideological underpinnings of terrorism. I am pleased to be back to build on those remarks. I also want to thank my former colleagues Matt Levitt and Michael Jacobson who continue to contribute to the scholarship on terrorism.

The institute should be proud of the continued series of high-level, national security–related discussions you have sponsored. In this most recent series of talks, you have heard from three key U.S. counterterrorism officials—Ambassador Dell Dailey, National Counterterrorism Center (NCTC) acting director Michael Leiter, and Treasury assistant secretary Pat O'Brien. I am honored to work with these leaders every day to prosecute the U.S. government's fight against al-Qaida and its like-minded allies.

From all of these speakers, you have heard about different dimensions of the comprehensive U.S. strategy to combat terrorism. Today, I would like to do three things: (1) highlight some counterterrorism innovations within the U.S. government; (2) discuss certain core markers of success we are witnessing in the war on terror; and (3) delineate the seminal challenges in bringing closure to the "long war."

Since 9/11, the president has laid out a clear strategy and vision—to wage a battle of arms and ideas—that has been implemented by thousands of men and women protecting our national and homeland security at home and abroad. It is an approach built on both an aggressive attack on the enemy and its ideology and a strong layered defense.

This integrated strategy is supported by a counterterrorism architecture built by this president and Congress to enable the U.S. government to win the war on terror in the long term. Now, we have in place the structures—like NCTC, the Department of Homeland Security, the Office of the Director of National Intelligence, NORTHCOM, DOJ's National Security Division, the FBI's National Security Branch, and Treasury's Office of Terrorism and Financial Intelligence (TFI)—that institutionalize the counterterrorism and homeland defense missions.

In addition, we have much of the legal framework—based on the Patriot Act, the Intelligence Reform and Terrorism Prevention Act (IRTPA), and other key administrative and legal provisions—to fight this long war effectively. A key piece of legislation—the modernization of the Foreign Intelligence Surveillance Act (FISA)—remains to be passed in Congress.

These efforts have had real-world effects and impact. In the first instance, they have saved lives. Along with our partners abroad, we have disrupted numerous al-Qaida-led and inspired plots, made countless terrorism-related arrests globally, and disrupted the logistical and financial networks of al-Qaida and its allies. The ongoing trial in London of the failed August 2006 airline plotters highlights the reality of the threats and disruptions plainly enough.

Counterterrorism Innovations

These efforts have allowed us to remain innovative and on the offense—along with our partners—against an adaptive transnational enemy. This innovation in our current strategy and approach has manifested itself in many ways.

- The information-sharing environment in which we now operate is vastly different from the one that existed just six years ago. The walls between intelligence and law enforcement, between federal, state, and local authorities, and even between foreign counterparts have fallen or been minimized in a way previously unimagined. In addition, more data is being gathered, shared, and analyzed. This has meant that more dots have and can be connected to identify suspect terrorist nodes, networks, and problematic trends.

- Today, the U.S. government's counterthreat response infrastructure—led by NCTC—is a system in which all of the key departments and agencies convene three times a day to review threats, once a week at the White House in the Counterterrorism Security Group to ensure we are addressing the high-level threats of concern, and then at the most senior levels of government when warranted. The president's daily intelligence briefings routinely include strategic and tactical terrorism matters, and he receives regular counterterrorism and homeland security updates from cabinet secretaries and agency heads. This system—with top-level attention—ensures constant focus on emerging or lingering threats of concern.

- We have built an interlocking system of defenses—extending our borders and homeland security. This starts with strong overseas partnerships and focused programs intended to prevent unwanted people and materials from reaching our shores—such as the Container Security Initiative, the Proliferation Security Initiative, and the Global Initiative to Combat Nuclear Terrorism. Such programs and relationships are backed by robust counterterrorist travel and screening efforts, which are then amplified by port and border security measures. This layer of defense is then backed by critical infrastructure protection in the homeland and joint partnerships with state, local, and tribal law enforcement. It is not just one part of our homeland defense that matters but instead the layered defense in depth that is critical to the success of this model—taking full advantage of international and local partnerships.

- This president has led the focus on preventing terrorists from acquiring, developing, or using weapons of mass destruction (WMD)—in particular nuclear weapons. He has laid out a six-part strategy, backed by an in-depth implementation plan and related programs, that links our counter-proliferation and counterterrorism efforts and communities into a comprehensive approach. This includes everything from protection of nuclear materials globally and radiological screening overseas to interdiction efforts and building capabilities to attribute the source of any such attack. This approach has led to innovations such as rethinking how we can deter or dissuade elements of terrorist networks. This includes undercutting the moral and religious legitimacy of the use of WMD by terrorists against innocents.

- Our counterterrorism strategy has depended on the use of all elements of national power, now integrated in a common planning document, the National Implementation Plan. Our approach has led to innovations in the use of our resources. This has included targeted development assistance with allies in safe havens of concerns and core capacity building with law enforcement, intelligence, and military counterparts to ensure our partners have the indigenous capabilities to fight the sources and symptoms of terrorism. It has also included creative deployment of our powers and suasion, as in the case of our use of targeted financial sanctions to identify and isolate rogue actors and to rely heavily on the international financial community in doing so.

- In our tactical and strategic engagement in the battle of ideas, we have adapted our approach to focus not just on defending the image of America and encouraging the underlying values of free societies but also attacking and undercutting the image and ideology of the enemy. This includes working with key allies—in governments and the private sector—to ensure the truth about al-Qaida's atrocities is revealed and understood. We are also connecting the private sector, NGOs, and interested parties to develop grassroots initiatives throughout the world that provide hope to youth and allow moderate networks to connect and defend against violent extremist ideologies. These are innovative projects intended to grow the grassroots countermovement that will counter extremist ideologues and their message.

These are just a handful of innovations and efforts that mark the everyday work of the U.S. government to implement our counterterrorism strategy. No doubt, improvements and further innovations need to be made, but we now have a U.S. counterterrorism architecture that allows us to fight the long war effectively, using all elements of national power.

While we implement this strategy, a key question that we must consistently ask ourselves is: Are we on the right track toward winning the war on terror?

I am paid to see and prevent the worst in the terrorism tea leaves. Sometimes daily setbacks or longer-term challenges appear to portend a protracted battle with a morphing enemy on numerous fronts. There may indeed be difficult streaks in the WOT, but I am also an optimist. I think we are now seeing important signs that mark progress in the war on terror and point to the eventual demise of al-Qaida.

Nature of the Enemy

To understand whether we are winning, one must understand the evolving nature of the enemy. We continue to face an enemy, led by al-Qaida, that is patient in its long-term strategic vision and willing to use any means to achieve its goals. Though its goals are global, it uses and co-opts local and cultural grievances and national movements and aspirations to fuel recruitment and establish its legitimacy. Their extremist and exclusive ideology preys on discontent and alienation, while providing a simple narrative that pretends to grant meaning and heroic outlet for the young. It is a terrorist movement that rejects elements of modernity while being fully devoted to using its implements, like the Internet.

Over the last three years, we have seen a hybrid face for this enemy emerge—with al-Qaida core leadership setting the strategic direction for the movement and often directing attack planning. At the same time, al-Qaida has aggressively and systematically moved to establish and use outposts, like al-Qaida in Iraq or al-Qaida in the Islamic Maghreb, that serve as forward bases for al-Qaida activity and strategic reach. In addition, al-Qaida has identified and nurtured pockets of radicalized cells or individuals in Western Europe with the capability to carry out deadly attacks under al-Qaida direction and in its name. Despite our disruptions and aggressive counterterrorism actions against al-Qaida leadership, this movement has found ways of extending its reach beyond the Afghanistan-Pakistan border region.

This is an enemy that is morphing in structure and adapting to changing geopolitical landscapes, but one that retains the same radical vision and ideology and devotion to the use of terrorism.

Markers of Success

Though this enemy appears to be reaching deeper into North Africa and Europe, there are a number of important developments that signal that al-Qaida and the movement it represents are under greater stress and finding more opposition to its program, in particular by Muslims affected directly by al-Qaida's tactics. The international environment for al-Qaida, including in Muslim majority countries, is growing more inhospitable.

There are some basic markers to note.

The consistent and frequent terrorist-related arrests being made—and underreported—around the world are an important signal of the growing seriousness with which countries take the threat. European services have arrested and disrupted numerous terrorist networks over the past year, to include operational cells wrapped up in Germany, Denmark, and Turkey. This is an indicator of both the awareness and growing effectiveness of countries' counterterrorism capabilities.

Countries are further addressing the counterterrorism threat themselves and with regional partners. This has entailed more than just classic counterterrorism work, to include more countries taking the field in the ideological battle space. This is seen most vividly in Southeast Asia, where the countries in the region have adopted full-fledged counterterrorism strategies—from "soft" counter-radicalization and jihadi rehabilitation programs to the development of "harder" special forces capabilities to address militants and terrorists on the battlefield. This approach and related regional partnerships signal an important graduation for the international community in reducing the global reach of the terrorist groups in the region.

Most importantly, there has been a growing rejection of the al-Qaida program and message. This is manifesting itself in several important ways.

- This is seen most vividly in Iraq, with the heart of al-Qaida's supposed constituency—the Sunni Arab tribes—openly and violently rejecting al-Qaida's presence and ideology. The Al-Anbar Awakening—with its broader ramifications for a rejection in the Arab heartland of al-Qaida itself—represents an existential threat to the al-Qaida program. Its long-term strategy of establishing an "Islamic Caliphate," galvanizing a broader anti-Western Muslim movement, and driving the United States out of the region stands at risk. Combined with our military surge and the tactical pressure we have put on anti-Coalition forces in Iraq, we have al-Qaida in retreat in Iraq. This is precisely why we have seen al-Qaida trying to regroup with targeted attacks on the tribal sheikhs and a flurry of messages from senior al-Qaida leadership about the need for unity and concentrated and primary effort in Iraq.

- Importantly, this rejection has started to emerge within extremist circles as well. Recently, former jihadist leaders of the Egyptian Islamic group published a series of books highly critical of jihadists and al-Qaida, to which Ayman al-Zawahiri has felt compelled to respond directly. The prominent Saudi cleric Shaykh Salman bin Fahd al-Awdah, who is well respected in extremist circles, condemned al-Qaida's actions and their impact on Islam in an open letter to Osama bin Laden, asking "How much blood has been spent? How many innocent people, children, elderly, and women have been killed, dispersed, or evicted in the name of al-Qaida?" And in London just yesterday, former extremists have launched the Quilliam Foundation, an organization dedicated to exposing and discrediting the ideology and voices of violent extremism.

- This rejection is not isolated to Iraq or to extremist circles. More and more Muslim and Arab populations—to include clerics and scholars—are questioning the value of al-Qaida's program and al-Qaida's fomenting of chaos and its justification for the killing of Muslim innocents. In an article published in the *Washington Post*, the Grand Mufti of Al-Azhar Mosque in Egypt noted that "attacking civilians, women, children, and the elderly by blowing oneself up is absolutely forbidden in Islam. No excuse can be made for the crimes committed in New York, Spain, and London, and anyone who tries to make excuses for these acts is ignorant of Islamic law, and their excuses are the result of extremism and ignorance." In October 2007, the Saudi Grand Mufti, Shaykh Abdul Aziz, delivered a speech warning Saudis not to undertake unauthorized jihadist activities and blamed "foreign elements" for exploiting the religious enthusiasm of young men for illegitimate purposes. The Grand Mufti also strongly warned wealthy Saudis to avoid funding causes that "harm Muslims." These are just some examples of concrete opposition to al-Qaida emerging around the world.

- It is significant that there is notable and consistent opposition in Arab country polling to the targeting of civilians and use of terrorism. As David Pollock recently noted in one of this institute's sessions, "Since 2004, the most striking new trend in regional opinion is the steady surge toward greater popular opposition to any attacks on American civilians anywhere among all Arab publics polled on such questions by different pollsters, many times over." This trend is reflected in popular culture. For example, popular musicians in Pakistan

Roughly Half of Americans Polled Believe the Nation and Its Allies Are Winning the War on Terror—Far Fewer Believe the Terrorists Are Winning

Who is winning the war on terror?

Year	Date	US/ Allies	Terrorists
2012	Jan 20–21	48%	17%
	Feb 20–21	51%	15%
	Mar 21–22	50%	17%
	Apr 30–May 1	51%	11%
	May 30–31	51%	16%
	July 9–10	47%	15%
	Aug 20–21	50%	20%
	Sep 23–24	45%	21%
2011	Jan 3–4	38%	30%
	Jan 31–Feb 1	39%	19%
	Mar 6–7	40%	24%
	Apr 7–8	32%	24%
	May 3–4	55%	11%
	June 6–8	50%	15%
	July 10–11	52%	13%
	Aug 9–10	44%	15%
	Sep 8–9	49%	13%
	Oct 8–9	46%	13%
	Nov 7–8	46%	14%
	Dec 12–13	50%	18%

TAKEN FROM: Rasmussen Reports, "War on Terror Update," September 26, 2012. www.rasmussenreports.com.

and Indonesia are performing antiterrorism songs that have become anthems for Muslims who want to distance themselves from extremism and violence. The tactics and methods of al-Qaida are more and more being rejected.

We know that all of this matters to al-Qaida and that its senior leadership is sensitive to the perceived legitimacy of both their actions and their ideology. They care about their image because it has real-world effects on recruitment, donations, and support in Muslim and religious communities for the al-Qaida message.

In his recent question and answer session, Zawahiri had to address the question of the legitimacy of targeting civilians. Interestingly, he sidestepped the question in part by claiming al-Qaida does not target civilians and arguing that loss of innocent Muslim life was either accidental or the Muslims mixing with non-Muslims were fair game. That is a hard argument to sell among the Muslim victims of al-Qaida terrorism in Baghdad, Riyadh, Casablanca, Amman, Algiers, and Istanbul. In fact, victims of al-Qaida terrorism are beginning to organize and are exposing the human toll of al-Qaida's tactics.

These challenges from within Muslim communities and even extremist circles will be insurmountable at the end of the day for al-Qaida for two fundamental reasons. Its baseline ideology to which its members are committed is violently exclusionary and the terrorist tactics with greatest potential strategic benefit to al-Qaida are precisely the ones that are most rejected and unpopular, including among Muslims.

Combined with the tactical and strategic "soft" and "hard" pressure placed on this movement by the international community, I believe that it is the moral pressure gaining momentum across the globe that will ultimately help dismantle al-Qaida. Al-Qaida's downfall and the end of the broader movement that it represents will follow inherently from their dark vision and terrorist tactics.

Persistent Challenges

This is not to say that the WOT is won or that we will not need to endure setbacks. Indeed, there are some critical challenges that we are attempting to address but that will require long-term commitments and attention from the U.S. government.

Senior al-Qaida leadership and trainees have found safe haven in the Pakistan/Afghanistan border area, in particular in Pakistan's Federally Administered Tribal Areas. This safe haven allows al-Qaida to plot and train, and provides a physical environment in which like-minded terrorist groups and operatives can mingle and create alliances of convenience. This is a direct threat to Pakistan, Afghanistan, and the rest of the world, given the planning and training occurring there every day.

We are engaged now with the new government in Islamabad to ensure they understand the criticality of this issue for us, and our commitment to working closely with them to ensure that the FATA does not remain in the long term an international terrorist safe haven. This is a complicated issue and part of the world, in which tribal dynamics dominate and in which the writ of the Pakistani central government does not extend. Our efforts with the Pakistanis include training and equipping their local, indigenous forces (the Frontier Corps) and the military, as well as providing development aid and economic assistance targeted to areas in need. This is part of an evolving, comprehensive strategy that will take time to succeed.

Indeed, the problem of the FATA safe haven will not be solved overnight, but it is clear that this is not just a Pakistani or American problem. It is one that affects the entire world and must involve key countries to help find solutions. For example, the British have pointed to numerous plots in the United Kingdom with direct links back to AQ in Pakistan. Coalition forces in Afghanistan and NATO countries have a direct interest in what happens in the FATA. We are addressing the need to internationalize the approach in fora like the

G8, in which the leaders have committed to working jointly with Pakistan to develop the FATA through economic assistance and investment.

In addition, the al-Qaida movement benefits from the seeming acceptance of a broader narrative that the "West" is at war with Islam, regardless of the reality that al-Qaida has led the slaughter of thousands of Muslim innocents around the world. Al-Qaida has artfully woven itself into the fabric of this narrative. We have difficulty breaking through this impression—regardless of the goodwill or efforts by the U.S. government and American citizens to help Muslims and non-Muslims alike as in the Pakistan earthquake, the South Asian tsunami, or even in the Balkans, and in Afghanistan. The cartoon incidents or isolated events and comments are often used by al-Qaida and their adherents to foment a greater sense of assault on the part of the West and values associated with broader globalization.

Part of the challenge is shifting this paradigm, so that the myth of such a conflict is debunked. Part of this is explaining that Muslims are a part of the "West" and breaking the notion of a clash of cultures. Even if we cannot affect this broad narrative quickly, we must ensure that al-Qaida is not portrayed as the defender or vanguard for Muslims. Al-Qaida and its ideology need to be divorced from this broader narrative and defined clearly as enemies of humanity who thrive on the misery and chaos they perpetuate, especially among Muslims. They should be revealed as themselves being at war with Muslims, especially those who do not believe as they do or subscribe to the al-Qaida agenda.

Much of this will require credible voices, outside of the U.S. government, to confront this false narrative. We are starting to see glimmers of precisely this, with some Muslims in Europe starting to reclaim what it means to be a faithful Muslim living in the "West." In response to the recent Geert Wilders' film *Fitna*, Dutch Muslims launched a viral "Hug

Wilders" campaign instead of reacting violently to the film. This is the type of action—if replicated in various communities and in different ways—that will help reframe the narrative and isolate violent extremists.

The international community is further hampered by a lack of consensus on what type of legal model and rules should apply to address the 21st-century terrorist threat represented by al-Qaida. What standards of proof, evidence, procedures, and sentences should apply against those who are trained or associated members of this loosely tied global terrorist movement intent on possibly using apocalyptic means to achieve their long-term strategic goals?

Clearly, this is not a classic criminal problem for which traditional criminal rules should apply, and the multiple theaters in which these terrorists operate make it difficult to apply any one standard or procedures. This legal and policy debate is starting to emerge in earnest in Europe, where the fixation to date has been on the U.S. attempts to fashion a legal construct and solution to address this problem. The international community—especially jurists and academics—need to engage in good faith to develop realistic options for a robust legal paradigm that allows for the protection of our national and collective security while respecting the rights of suspected individuals.

Finally, Iran and Syria's state sponsorship of terrorism presents immediate challenges to our counterterrorism policies and national security. We know that Iran's Islamic Revolutionary Guard Corps (IRGC) Qods Force supports terrorism around the world—and has done so historically in Lebanon and in attacks such as the bombing of the Argentine-Israeli Mutual Association (AMIA) in Buenos Aires in 1994. This assistance is not restricted to Hizballah and the Palestinian rejectionist groups. We know that the Qods Force provides weapons and financial support to the Taliban to support anti-

U.S. and anti-Coalition activity in Afghanistan, as well as to Iraqi Shi'a who target and kill Coalition and Iraqi forces.

With Syria, we know that it continues to be a center for terrorist activity, including serving as the primary pipeline for foreign suicide bombers into Iraq through the Damascus airport. These suicide bombers represent a strategically important threat to Iraq's stability and the safety of Iraqi civilians and our soldiers. We need to continue to pressure and expose the ongoing state sponsorship of these two regimes, which have an interest in not only opposing U.S. interests but in sowing instability wherever they see an advantage for their interests.

Such state sponsorship is dangerous because these countries provide weapons, training, financing, and logistical support to unaccountable terrorist actors. Such sponsorship also provides some legitimacy to those still wedded to the dying orthodoxy that terrorist acts can be justified.

Conclusion

We are attempting to address all of these challenges with the varied tools at our command and by innovating new areas in our counterterrorism approach. We know the war on terror—with its embedded struggle against a violent extremist ideology—is a generational calling that requires the entire U.S. government and the international community to act. There will be challenges and setbacks, but there is no doubt in my mind that we will see victory in this struggle, with markers and key indicators of that success emerging even today. There is also no doubt that we will see al-Qaida defeated, imploding from its own moral hypocrisy and strategic missteps. That said, we must remain focused and committed to ensuring the safety and security of this country against an enemy that remains committed to the destruction of our way of life. That has been the work of this administration, and it will no doubt be the work of administrations to come.

"If some historian of the future should attempt to chronicle the decline of the American republic, the point when history made its fateful turn will be readily identifiable: September 11, 2001."

America Is Losing the War on Terror

Justin Raimondo

Justin Raimondo is a libertarian author and editorial director of Antiwar.com, a website opposing military imperialism. In the following viewpoint, Raimondo insists that America is losing the war on terrorism. According to him, al Qaeda—the terrorists responsible for the September 11, 2001, attacks on America—can easily and cheaply spread terror and manipulate US responses, forcing Washington to spend billions of dollars to safeguard the country and track down suspects. In this way, al Qaeda can bleed the United States economically and sap its will to keep up an ongoing war on multiple fronts—including a vulnerable home front, Raimondo contends. He warns that by battling an elusive enemy, restricting freedoms in the name of fighting terror, and inviting backlash from the Islamic world, the US government is damaging America's credibility and heading the country toward defeat.

As you read, consider the following questions:

1. Why does Raimondo think the increase in "chatter" on terrorist communications networks is not a credible way to define clear threats?

2. According to the author, how does the Obama administration hope to inoculate the Middle East and North Africa against al Qaeda?

3. As opposed to large-scale invasion and democracy building, what tactic does Raimondo claim was responsible for finding and "nailing" Osama bin Laden?

New York is a city under siege. As I write on the morning of the tenth anniversary of 9/11 [that is, on September 11, 2011], thousands of police, federal agents, and the National Guard are swarming over the panicked metropolis, as reports proliferate that three suspected terrorists who entered the country recently are planning a car-bomb attack. Bomb-sniffing dogs patrol Grand Central Station, while police checkpoints delay traffic for hours—and threats appear on the White House Facebook page.

Amid the hundreds of editorials, reminiscences, and opinion pieces directed our way this somber day, all of which seek to extract some larger meaning from the worst terrorist attack in American history, the real meaning of that signal event is plain as day: We are losing the "war on terrorism"—big time.

Bleeding America

Look at what happened in New York City: How many resources, how many tax dollars, have been expended in the search for three terrorists who may or may not be planning an attack? One of the major pieces of evidence for the 9/11/11 plot is the uptick in "chatter" supposedly filling the terrorist communications network. But what if this "chatter" is a calculated tactic? Simply by feinting—"leaking" false information— the Bad Guys can provoke a major and exhausting response, draining us until we're eventually so worn down—or so bankrupt—that they accomplish their goal without even launching another strike on the scale of 9/11.

As [al-Qaeda terrorist leader] Osama bin Laden put it in a videotaped message broadcast by Al Jazeera on November 1, 2004:

"All that we have to do is to send two mujahedin [Islamic freedom fighters] to the farthest point East to raise a piece of cloth on which is written al-Qa'ida in order to make the generals race there to cause America to suffer human economic and political losses without their achieving for it anything of note. . . . So we are continuing this policy in bleeding America to the point of bankruptcy."

The late terrorist leader went on to point out that

"Al-Qa'ida spent $500,000 on the [9/11 attacks], while America in the incident and its aftermath lost—according to the lowest estimates—more than 500 billion dollars, meaning that every dollar of al-Qa'ida defeated a million dollars by the permission of Allah besides the loss of a huge number of jobs. As for the size of the economic deficit, it has reached record, astronomical numbers estimated to total more than a trillion dollars. And even more dangerous and bitter for America is that the mujahedin recently forced [President George W.] Bush to resort to emergency funds to continue the fight in Afghanistan and Iraq which is evidence of the success of the bleed-until-bankruptcy plan with Allah's permission."

As we scramble to defend New York City against a threat that may not even exist, bin Laden's ghost is laughing at us from beyond the grave [i.e., he was killed by US troops in 2011].

Losing Freedom Under a Policy of Perpetual War

Yet there are worse fates than mere bankruptcy. We are living in a world where, if you get up and go to the bathroom more than once while traveling on an airplane, the flight is diverted on account of your "suspicious behavior."

Hysteria has blinded us to the real threat. Even as the terrorists openly proclaim their "bleed-until-bankruptcy plan," we continue to travel down the same path to economic oblivion. It has been widely noted that the 19 hijackers appropriated our own high technology—airliners—and turned them against us, but little noted that they also appropriated our emotional commitment to a war of revenge and used it in a similar fashion. As bin Laden put it:

> "So we are continuing this policy in bleeding America to the point of bankruptcy. Allah is willing and nothing is too great for Allah. That being said, those who say that al-Qa'ida has won against the administration in the White House or that the administration has lost in this war have not been precise because when one scrutinizes the results, one cannot say that al-Qa'ida is the sole factor in achieving these spectacular gains. Rather, the policy of the White House that demands the opening of war fronts to keep busy their various corporations—whether they be working in the field of arms or oil or reconstruction—has helped al-Qa'ida to achieve those enormous results."

New fronts in our endless "war on terrorism" are opened, it seems, with each passing week: Somalia, Sudan, Yemen, the Philippines, Pakistan, and now Libya—where we are carrying out the new co-optation strategy of the [Barack] Obama administration, which seeks to hijack the "Arab Spring" [protests in Arab countries against oppressive governments beginning in 2010] and utilize it as a weapon against Islamist extremism. By setting up US-aligned "democratic" states in the Middle

East, from Egypt to Libya and beyond, the Americans hope to inoculate the region against the virus represented by al-Qaeda.

This is a dangerous policy in so many ways that it would take more than a single column to even list them. Suffice to say that recent events in Egypt, and the growing influence of Islamist elements among the Libyan rebels, underscores how the "blowback" from our efforts could backfire in our faces.

We've spent trillions fighting this losing battle, but more than money has been lost—we've forfeited our freedom. The barrage of legislation enacted since 9/11 that empowers our government to openly spy on us in ways that would have been inconceivable before has effectively abolished our old republic, and replaced it with something else—a misshapen, polyglot creature, half "democratic" and fully authoritarian, which cannot sustain itself economically, and—for all its vaunting about exercising "world leadership"—shows every sign of descending into an irreversible decline.

The "War Party" Is Leading America to Disaster

If some historian of the future should attempt to chronicle the decline of the American republic, the point when history made its fateful turn will be readily identifiable: September 11, 2001, the day the 9/11 coup d'etat was victorious. As President George W. Bush sat reading *The Pet Goat* to a group of school-children while the World Trade Center and the Pentagon came under attack, the government was effectively taken over by Vice President Dick Cheney and a cabal of government officials already in place and ready to assume command of the world's mightiest superpower. From that moment on, the War Party had its hands on the reins of power, and they remain in the driver's seat to this day—albeit under another partisan alias.

Estimated War Funding by Operation: FY2001–FY2012 War Request

(in billions of dollars of budget authority)

Operation and Source of Funds	FY01 & FY02	FY03	FY04	FY05	FY06	FY07	FY08	FY09	FY10	FY11	FY12 Request
Iraq	0.0	53.0	75.9	85.5	101.6	131.2	142.1	95.5	71.3	49.3	17.7
Afghanistan	20.8	14.7	14.5	20.0	19.0	39.2	43.5	59.5	93.8	118.6	113.7
Enhanced security	13.0	8.0	3.7	2.1	0.8	0.5	0.1	0.1	0.1	0.1	0.1
Unallocated	0.0	5.5	0.0	0.0	0.0	0.0	0.0	0.0	0.0	0.0	0.0
Total	33.8	81.2	94.1	107.6	121.4	170.9	185.7	155.1	165.3	168.1	131.7
Annual change	NA	140%	16%	13%	13%	41%	9%	−16%	7%	2%	−22%
Change since FY03	NA	NA	16%	33%	50%	111%	129%	91%	104%	107%	62%

TAKEN FROM: Amy Belasco, "The Cost of Iraq, Afghanistan, and Other Global War on Terror Operations Since 9/11," Congressional Research Service, March 29, 2011.

For ten years they've been driving this country into the ground, just as bin Laden predicted they would. As dead as he is, he's having the last laugh: His strategy is working.

Speaking of strategies that work: The circumstances surrounding the terrorist icon's death point the way to fighting an effective campaign against those who plot and plan to pull off another 9/11. We didn't get bin Laden by launching a massive invasion, or by "democratizing" the Middle East: It was good old-fashioned police work, meticulous and patiently executed, that finally nailed him in his lair. We didn't beat the Mafia by invading Italy—and we won't beat the Islamist Mafioso by conquering Afghanistan and occupying great swathes of the Muslim world. Unfortunately, our present rulers show no signs of having learned the lesson of their greatest success.

Yes, we do have enemies who want to kill us, but those ghouls who worship Thanatos [death] understand that death can take on many forms. A man can still continue to exist long after he has betrayed everything that made him uniquely himself. Nations, too, can commit this kind of slow-motion suicide, so that the passage from life to death can go undetected until it is far too late to reverse course.

Is it too late for us? I fear the answer to this question, because we cannot know it until that point is well behind us. I can only let the historians of the future argue the question, while here, in the present, I fight—in my small way—to influence their verdict.

"The immediate physical threat posed by al-Qaeda has diminished greatly over the past ten years."

Al Qaeda Has Failed and Its Threat Defeated

William McCants and William Rosenau

In the following viewpoint, William McCants and William Rosenau contend that the Islamic terrorist organization al Qaeda has been defeated. McCants and Rosenau claim al Qaeda has not pulled off another grand-scale attack on American soil since September 11, 2001. Indeed, the pair insists the insurrectionist aims of al Qaeda never materialized, and its leaders are now dead or on the run. McCants and Rosenau believe it is time to declare victory and refocus US energies on refining the tools and strategies that led to success in the war on terror. William Mc-Cants and William Rosenau are research analysts at CNA Strategic Studies, a nonprofit research and analysis center. Both formerly served as policy advisors in the Office of the Coordinator for Counterterrorism at the US Department of State.

As you read, consider the following questions:

1. What evidence do McCants and Rosenau present to show al Qaeda failed to achieve one of its "paramount political objectives" in the Arab world?

2. Why do the authors believe sending positive messages about the United States throughout Islamic lands is a tactic worth dropping from the counterterrorism tool kit?

3. What do the authors argue has been the "most powerful weapon" in preventing terrorist attacks?

Ten years into our struggle against al-Qaeda, it's time to acknowledge that the "war" is over and recognize that the United States and its international partners overreacted to the al-Qaeda threat. Terrorism, after all, is designed to elicit such overreactions. But the confluence of the recent death of [al-Qaeda leader Osama] bin Laden, harsh new economic realities, the democratic movements in the Middle East, and the ten-year anniversary of the September 11 [2001] attacks provide an ideal time to take stock of what it actually takes to deal with the al-Qaeda threat.

The Failure of Al-Qaeda

The immediate physical threat posed by al-Qaeda has diminished greatly over the past ten years. The elimination of Osama bin Laden—a long-overdue counterterrorism triumph—and the relentless dismantling of al-Qaeda's senior leadership in their Pakistani sanctuaries and redoubts are obvious but powerful signs of the enterprise's darkening prospects. The recent [August 2011] death of one of al-Qaeda's most capable and influential senior leaders, Abu Abd al-Rahman Atiyatallah, in an alleged U.S. drone attack in Pakistan, will only hasten its leadership's collapse.

More important, al-Qaeda has failed utterly in its efforts to achieve one of its paramount political objectives. From the

19th century through the present day, terrorists and insurgents—from transatlantic anarchists to Fanonists of the tiers monde to Nepalese Maoists—have spun insurrectionist fantasies of taking over. But the Salafist-jihadists' worldwide Islamic uprising, against perceived enemies of the faith, never materialized. The Muslim masses have refused to play their part in the al-Qaeda dramaturgy. The terrorism intended to generate widespread rebellion has failed to arouse a global Muslim community. Most damningly, al-Qaeda has been irrelevant to the popular uprisings sweeping the heartland of the Muslim world [from 2010–2012].

Rethinking How America Fights Terrorism

In recognizing al-Qaeda's failures and weaknesses, we should reevaluate the political, military, economic, and other instruments the United States wields against terrorism. Three of these methods need particular scrutiny.

The first is social and economic development. It might be useful in dealing with large-scale insurgencies, but development is unlikely to address the idiosyncratic motives of the small number of people who join terrorist groups. It's true that addressing the "root causes" of terrorism sounds like a sensible, systemic course of action, but few truly agree what those causes are—nor is there anything like a consensus on what measures are likely to prove most effective.

The second questionable tool is one used in part of a broader set of information operations: positive messaging about the United States. There are excellent reasons to pursue public diplomacy, but countering terrorism is not one of them. The young people who are vulnerable to al-Qaeda's recruitment pitches are likely to be impervious to positive messages about the United States. In addition, linking public diplomacy with counterterrorism risks alienating intended audiences, which can easily detect the fear and hidden agenda lurking behind the friendly American smile. The United States needs to dissuade people from attacking its citizens—but those people do not need to like the United States in order to abandon violence.

The third tool to drop is the one with which we've had the least success: occupying the country from which a terrorist group is attempting to recruit. There might be good reasons to invade and occupy a country, but eliminating a terrorist group is not one of them. It only engenders new recruits for the terrorists' cause and it provides them a fertile training ground. Moreover, it plays into al-Qaeda's openly professed strategy of bleeding U.S. resources to force it to reduce its influence in the Middle East.

What Works in Counterterrorism

What's left in the counterterrorist's tool kit? Most of the significant advances against al-Qaeda and its fellow travelers over the last ten years have come as a consequence of intelligence gathering, good policing, spreading the awful truth about al-Qaeda, and helping other governments do these same things. These are not ancillary to counterterrorism but rather its essential components.

Violent operations against al-Qaeda have garnered most of the public's attention. But, in terms of preventing terrorist attacks, the most powerful weapon has been decidedly unglamorous and much less visible: police work informed by well-placed sources inside terrorist cells. Major plots in New York, London, Stockholm, and other key urban centers have been foiled by police, often working in unison with intelligence services. Assisting foreign police forces should be a major component of the U.S. counterterrorism repertoire—but such aid is limited by considerable restrictions from Congress and a lack of skilled police trainers able and willing to work abroad.

Eliminating terrorist networks is not enough. They also have to be discredited among the audiences they seek to influence. Although it is true that al-Qaeda has done much to dis-

Al-Qaeda's Declining Significance

Over the course of the 10 years [September 2001 to September 2011], American authorities foiled more than two dozen al-Qaeda plots. Those averted tragedies were not foremost on the minds of revelers who gathered to celebrate [al-Qaeda leader Osama] bin Laden's demise on May 1 [2011] at Ground Zero, Times Square, and in front of the White House. But if a mere few of the plots had materialized, those spaces might not even have been open to public assembly.

Not only have U.S. authorities managed to keep America safe from al-Qaeda for a decade; by the time he was killed, Osama bin Laden was barely a leader. Among the items recovered at his compound in Abbottabad [Pakistan] were some recent writings, in which the former icon lamented al-Qaeda's dramatically sinking stock and pondered organizational rebranding as a possible antidote.

His growing insignificance as a global player was not the product of chance. The marginalization of the world's principal jihadist was the result of audacious American policy—indeed, the most controversial and hotly debated policy undertaken in the wake of 9/11 [referring to the September 11, 2001, terrorist attacks on the United States].

Abe Greenwald,
"What We Got Right in the War on Terror,"
Commentary, *September 2011.*

credit itself through its doctrinal and operational excesses—killing civilians, attacking places of worship, targeting fellow Muslims—the U.S. and its allies have done an excellent job of magnifying those excesses. Two effective techniques have been releasing private correspondence between al-Qaeda's senior leaders, which is rarely flattering, and quietly pointing the media to evidence that al-Qaeda does not represent the aspirations of the vast majority of Muslims.

Not only has the U.S. become adept at using these tools, it has also been skillful in showing others how to use them. For example, Indonesia, once a fertile ground for militant Islamist activity, is now a counterterrorism success story because of these efforts.

Given the considerable damage that "kinetic" military operations have reportedly done to al-Qaeda, military and paramilitary force should obviously remain an important part of the counterterrorist arsenal. But it should be reserved only for killing the most senior leaders and operatives in a terrorist organization—those whose skills are most lethal and most difficult to replace—and only when local security forces are unable or unwilling to take appropriate action. This does not require occupying a country, but rather cultivating local allies and spending money to develop intelligence networks.

The War Is Over

There will inevitably one day be another large attack on American soil and the U.S. government will inevitably overreact. That is the response terrorism is designed to elicit and the United States, because its safety and isolation make terrorism feel so horrifying, is particularly susceptible to such a response. But if Washington can use this 10-year landmark to throw out the counterterrorism tools that haven't worked and to sharpen the ones that do, the negative consequences of that overreaction will be minimal. If not, the United States will have drawn the wrong lessons from the last ten years, obliging its terrorist enemies by repeating its worst mistakes.

| *"Al Qaeda is far from dead. Acting as if it were will not make it so."*

Al Qaeda Has Not Been Defeated

Seth G. Jones

Seth G. Jones is a senior political scientist at the RAND Corporation and a former senior advisor at US Special Operations Command. He is the author of Hunting in the Shadows: The Pursuit of al Qa'ida Since 9/11. *In the following viewpoint, Jones insists that it is premature to consider the terrorist group al Qaeda a diminished threat. Although Jones believes America and its allies have made progress in disrupting the organization, he argues that al Qaeda is still recruiting vast numbers of operatives, building alliances in Islamic nations, and carrying out attacks against its perceived enemies. Jones claims that the US government cannot afford to shift the focus away from this dangerous group.*

As you read, consider the following questions:

1. What is al Shabaab, as Jones describes it?

2. According to Jones, how many attacks has al Qaeda made in Iraq since the death of Osama bin Laden?

3. To what region of the globe is President Barack Obama shifting America's military operations, as Jones reports?

A year after U.S. forces killed Osama bin Laden [in May 2011], most policy makers and pundits believe al Qaeda is near collapse. "Another nail in the coffin," one senior U.S. official told me after the death of an al Qaeda operative in Pakistan last month [March 2012] from a U.S. drone strike. In testimony before the Senate in February, Director of National Intelligence James Clapper said the core al Qaeda is likely becoming of "symbolic importance."

This conclusion is presumptuous. As the administration looks eastward—a strategy that incorporates China's rise—underestimating al Qaeda would be a dangerous mistake. With a handful of regimes teetering from the Arab Spring [protests in Arab countries against oppressive governments beginning in 2010], al Qaeda is pushing into the vacuum and riding a resurgent wave as its affiliates engage in a violent campaign of attacks across the Middle East and North Africa.

Strengthening Al Qaeda's Influence in the Arab World

Take a look around the Arab world.

In Yemen, al Qaeda in the Arabian Peninsula has increased control in such provinces as Shabwah and Abyan, as the central government in Sana [the capital of Yemen] faces a leadership crisis and multiple insurgencies. From this sanctuary, al Qaeda continues to plot attacks against the U.S. homeland, according to U.S. government assessments, ranging from plans for bombs hidden in cameras and printer cartridges to ones surgically implanted in humans and animals.

Across the Gulf of Aden in Somalia, militants of the al Qaeda affiliate al Shabaab bombarded the city of Baidoa in

April, trying to expand their foothold in southern portions of the country. With a growing number of American citizens from cities like Minneapolis and Phoenix traveling to—and from—Somalia to fight alongside al Shabaab, there is an increasing likelihood that radicalized operatives could perpetrate an attack in the United States. A report last year by the House Committee on Homeland Security found that al Shabaab had recruited at least 40 Somali Americans from immigrant communities in the U.S.

Another trend pointing to al Qaeda's resurgence is the size of its global network. Since Sept. 11, 2001, it has expanded the number of affiliated groups. Along with Somalia's al Shabaab, they now include al Qaeda in Iraq—which is increasing its foothold in Baghdad, Diyala and Saladin provinces. Also active are al Qaeda in the Arabian Peninsula and, in North Africa, al Qaeda in the Islamic Maghreb. The leaders of these affiliates have sworn *bayat*, or loyalty, to al Qaeda leader Ayman al-Zawahiri and provided him with funding, global influence, and a cadre of trained fighters. None of these organizations existed a decade ago.

Al Qaeda has also established relationships with a growing number of allied groups such as the Pakistani Taliban, Pakistan's Lashkar-e-Taiba and Nigeria's Boko Haram. While these are not formal members of al Qaeda, a loose arrangement allows them to cooperate with al Qaeda for specific operations or training when their interests converge. And several of them—the Tehrik-e-Taliban Pakistan and Lashkar-e-Taiba—have been actively recruiting in the U.S.

New Leadership

As for al Qaeda's own leadership in Pakistan—it is not dead, despite claims from some U.S. officials. Ayman al-Zawahiri took over as leader of al Qaeda after bin Laden's death, and Abu Yahya al-Libi, the head of al Qaeda's religious committee, became his deputy. They are flanked by a new cast of opera-

Al Qaeda's Infrastructure Is Intact

Reading jihadi publications, one finds dozens of former militant commanders from campaigns of the 1980s and 1990s—Afghanistan, Bosnia, Chechnya, Kashmir—who continue to provide advice to the movement, guidance on training and tactics, and a seemingly perpetual source of open-source written material that offers lessons for adapting to the enemy's capabilities. Beyond these, there are dozens of highly qualified scholars who provide the religious justification for targeting and killing declared enemies. None of this infrastructure and intellectual framework has been weakened in any meaningful way during the last 10 years of warfare against al Qaeda.

Christopher Heffelfinger, "Mission Not Accomplished," Foreign Policy, *August 5, 2011. www.foreignpolicy.com.*

tives such as Hamza al-Ghamdi (a top facilitator for Zawahiri), Abd al-Rahman al-Maghrebi (media committee), and Abu-Zaid al-Kuwaiti (religious committee).

To be sure, security concerns have prohibited al Qaeda's central shura, or council, from playing a major strategic and operational role overseas, at least for the moment. The shura can't meet as a group anymore and its members spend an inordinate amount of time simply trying to survive. Yet as America's relationship with Pakistan continues to deteriorate, how long will the U.S. be able to pressure a state whose intelligence service has ties with some of al Qaeda's allies, such as the Haqqani network and Lashkar-e-Taiba?

Increasing Number of Al Qaeda Attacks

Finally, there is the fact that attacks by al Qaeda and its affiliates have increased over the past several years, according to data from the Global Terrorism Database at the University of Maryland. Even since bin Laden's death, al Qaeda affiliates have maintained a steady operational tempo. According to U.S. government data, al Qaeda in Iraq has conducted more than 200 attacks and killed more than a thousand Iraqis since the bin Laden raid—a jump from the previous year.

Despite all this evidence that al Qaeda is regrouping, the [Barack] Obama administration is turning its attention toward the Far East. It has pulled U.S. military forces out of Iraq and plans to have them out of Afghanistan in 2014. The first tranche of Marines to be withdrawn from Afghanistan has already landed in Australia as part of America's most significant expansion in the Pacific since the end of the Vietnam War. The Department of Defense's new strategic guidance, released in January with a foreword by President Obama, concludes that the U.S. will continue to conduct some counterterrorism but now "rebalance toward the Asian-Pacific region."

Addressing U.S. interests in the Far East is important, but not if it means losing focus on America's most pressing danger zone: the arc running from North Africa to the Middle East and South Asia that is the heart of al Qaeda's territory. In Afghanistan and Pakistan, U.S. special operations and other combat forces will be needed to target militants and train Afghan forces well after 2014. The same is true in Yemen, Somalia and other countries across the region, where U.S. forces—especially clandestine special operations, intelligence units and law enforcement—just play a critical, long-term role in targeting al Qaeda and building local capacity.

Al Qaeda is far from dead. Acting as if it were will not make it so.

"This is the moment . . . to begin to seek ways to defend America even while guiding us back to our true self: a country with respect for the law, restraint when it comes to the use of force, and rights for all."

America Must End the War on Terror to Reestablish Its Regard for Law

Karen J. Greenberg

In the following viewpoint, Karen J. Greenberg attests that the killing of al Qaeda terrorist leader Osama bin Laden in 2011 should mark the end of America's war on terrorism and a rebirth of the country's respect for law. In her opinion, Washington should release prisoners held indefinitely in detention, begin prosecuting accusations of torture conducted by US personnel, and return the responsibility of trying suspected terrorists back to the capable hands of the courts. Greenberg believes that these acts will show that America upholds the ideals of justice while not sacrificing its determination to protect its citizens from harm.

Karen J. Greenberg is the executive director of the New York University Center on Law and Security and the author of The Least Worst Place: Guantanamo's First 100 Days.

As you read, consider the following questions:

1. Greenberg claims the detention of John Walker Lindh was revenge for what event?

2. How does Greenberg envision the work of a rehabilitation program for detainees captured during the war on terror?

3. According to the author, the Justice Department has been deprived of trying what kind of terrorist suspects?

In the seven weeks since the killing of [al-Qaeda leader] Osama bin Laden [on May 2, 2011], pundits and experts of many stripes have concluded that his death represents a marker of genuine significance in the story of America's encounter with terrorism. [National security analyst for CNN] Peter Bergen, a bin Laden expert, was typically blunt the day after the death when he wrote, "Killing bin Laden is the end of the war on terror. We can just sort of announce that right now."

Yet you wouldn't know it in Washington where, if anything, the [Barack] Obama administration and Congress have interpreted the killing of al-Qaeda's leader as a virtual license to double down on every "front" in the war on terror. Secretary of State Hillary Clinton was no less blunt than Bergen, but with quite a different end point in mind. "Even as we mark this milestone," she said on the day Bergen's comments were published, "we should not forget that the battle to stop al-Qaeda and its syndicate of terror will not end with the death of bin Laden. Indeed, we must take this opportunity to renew our resolve and redouble our efforts."

National security adviser John Brennan concurred. "This is a strategic blow to al-Qaeda," he commented in a White House press briefing. "It is a necessary but not necessarily sufficient blow to lead to its demise. But we are determined to destroy it." Similarly, at his confirmation hearings to become secretary of defense, CIA [Central Intelligence Agency] director Leon Panetta called for Washington to expand its shadow wars. "We've got to keep the pressure up," he told the senators.

As if to underscore the policy implications of this commitment to "redoubling our efforts," drone aircraft were dispatched on escalating post–bin Laden assassination runs from Yemen (including a May 6th failed attempt on American al-Qaeda follower Anwar al-Awlaki) to Pakistan. There, on May 23rd, a drone failed to take out Taliban leader Mullah Omar, while, on June 2nd, an attempt to kill Ilyas Kashmiri, a militant associated with the 2008 terrorist attack on Mumbai, India, may (or may not) have failed. And those were only the most publicized of escalating drone attacks, while reports of a major "intensification" of the drone campaign in Yemen are pouring in.

Renewing the War or Terror

In the meantime, President Obama used the bin Laden moment to push through and sign into law a four-year renewal of the Patriot Act [also known as the USA PATRIOT Act], despite bipartisan resistance in Congress and the reservations of civil liberties groups. They had stalled its passage earlier in the year, hoping to curtail some of its particularly onerous sections, including the "lone wolf" provision that allows surveillance of non-US citizens in America, even if they have no ties to foreign powers, and the notorious Section 215, which grants the FBI [Federal Bureau of Investigation] authority to obtain library and business records in the name of national security.

One thing could not be doubted. The administration was visibly using the bin Laden moment to renew George W. Bush's global war on terror (even if without that moniker). And let's not forget about the leaders of Congress, who promptly accelerated their efforts to ensure that the apparatus for the war that 9/11 [referring to the September 11, 2001, terrorist attacks on the United States] started would never die. Congressman Howard McKeon (R-CA), chairman of the House Armed Services Committee, was typical. On May 9th, he introduced legislation meant to embed in law the principle of indefinite detention without trial for suspected terrorists until "the end of hostilities." What this would mean, in reality, is the perpetuation *ad infinitum* of that Bush-era creation, our prison complex at Guantánamo (not to speak of our second Guantánamo at Bagram air base in Afghanistan).

In other words, Washington now seems to be engaged in a wholesale post–bin Laden ratification of business as usual, but this time on steroids. . . .

Pause to Consider a New Direction

But think about it for a moment: Should the postmortem to bin Laden be just a continuation of the same old same old? Shouldn't there be a national pause for reflection as the tenth anniversary of 9/11 approaches? Wouldn't it make sense to stop and rethink policy in the light of his death and of a visibly tumultuous new moment in the Greater Middle East with its various uprisings and brewing civil wars?

Why has an administration that prides itself on thinking before doing pushed on without a moment's reflection? Why shouldn't the president establish a commission filled with at least a few new faces (and so a few new thoughts) to assess what a war on terror might even mean today? And why not insist that, until the findings of such a commission come in, there will be no new expenditures, legislation, or policy decisions to continue—let alone further expand—that war, its detention policies, or for that matter the Patriot Act?

Were the president to establish such a commission, here are five symbolic steps it might recommend—hardly the only ones, but a start—that could help set the U.S. on another path and put the war on terror behind us:

1. Concede that there is no more tangible end point for the war on terror than the death of bin Laden: Rather than trying to banish the term "war on terror" (as the Obama administration did in 2009), let's face it squarely. Practically speaking, at the moment as for the past near decade, it is little but a catch-all phrase for "endless war."

Our commission would have to face a basic question: If we are not to commit to war without end, what could the "cessation of hostilities" possibly mean when it comes to American terror policy? Any attempt at a definition would have to grapple with the real meaning of bin Laden's death. After all, it may be the only tangible victory we'll ever have. What a moment, then, to announce that the war on terror has now passed out of its "war" phase and entered a phase of risk management.

At present, Congress is considering an expansion of the Authorization [for] Use [of] Military Force (AUMF) that it passed on September 14, 2001, and that allowed "the use of force against those nations, organizations, or persons [the president] determines planned, authorized, committed, or aided" the attacks of 9/11. The current version builds upon the previous open-ended war model and actually expands the number of possible targets for the use of force to those who "have engaged in hostilities or have directly supported hostilities in aid of a nation, organization or person" that is engaged in hostilities against the U.S. or its coalition partners. [The act was signed into law in December 2011 as the National Defense Authorization Act for Fiscal Year 2012].

Nor does it have an end date. How long this overly broad, overly vague policy would remain in effect remains unknown. It would be far better if current and pending revisions of the AUMF were more honest in acknowledging that the counterterrorism policy it promotes is slated to last indefinitely, much like the "wars" on drugs and organized crime. This would, at least, put in front of lawmakers the appropriate question: Are you willing to authorize military force as your perpetual state of risk management against an ever-expanding list of enemies? Perhaps, in the context of an endless state of war (and the expenses that would go with it), Congress might prove more circumspect about granting such broad powers to the president.

Releasing Prisoners of the War

2. Release John Walker Lindh: This would be a symbolic act of compassion, a way to turn our attention back to the first moments of the Bush administration's disastrous global war on terror, and perhaps help along the process of heading Washington in new directions. Lindh, you may remember, was the young man captured and turned over to U.S. forces by Afghan allies in the early weeks of the invasion of Afghanistan.

An American who had spent time with the Taliban and was ready to fight for them (but not against the United States), he was the first person against whom the Bush administration, in one of their favored phrases, "took off the gloves." He was mistreated and abused while wounded. Later, faced with the prospect of never emerging from jail, he provided information to the authorities in exchange for a 20-year sentence in a plea deal.

Even George W. Bush described him as a "poor boy" who had been "misled," an upper-middle-class American kid whose teenage identity issues sent him deep into the fundamentalist part of the Muslim world, though with no indication on his part of any interest in *jihad*, nor the slightest idea that the United States would invade Afghanistan and he would find himself on the other side of the lines from his own countrymen.

Lindh's mistreatment in Afghanistan and subsequent sentencing here were essentially acts of symbolic revenge for the tragic death of CIA agent Mike Spann, the first official American casualty in what was already being called the global war on terror. [He died during an insurgent riot in Afghanistan in November 2001.] His sentence was also meant as a warning to others who might consider his path. . . .

Lindh's release would be a signal that the United States was ready to return to an era of calm justice and that the war on terror, with all its excesses, was truly coming to an end.

3. Create a rehabilitation program for releasing Guantánamo detainees currently assigned to indefinite detention: In the same spirit, it's time to signal that, along with the war on terror, the paroxysm of fears that led us to detain individuals who had not committed crimes, but were otherwise deemed harmful, has come to an end. The Obama administration's most recent directive on Guantánamo follows its long-hinted-at intention to hold approximately four dozen Guantánamo detainees in indefinite detention for a variety of reasons. Bottom line: Although there is insufficient evidence to convict them, administration officials have determined that each of them could pose a danger to this country, if released.

Under U.S. law, detention without trial poses constitutional problems, which is why Guantánamo detainees were granted *habeas corpus* rights by the Supreme Court. Similarly, under the laws of war, the detention of prisoners is only justified while hostilities are ongoing. If there really is no "war" on terror, it is hard to justify holding detainees indefinitely without a fair adjudication of their rights in a court of law.

Why not, then, consider creating an American version of the de-radicalization or rehabilitation programs that flourish elsewhere in the world—notably, for example in Indonesia—as a prelude to release for those where the evidence for a trial is absent? A rehabilitation program might steer individuals toward nonviolent behavior, whatever their ideological leanings; it might reeducate them on the subject of Islam; it might introduce notions of rights and liberties. Religious leaders, psychologists, and counterterrorism officials could fashion such a program jointly as they do elsewhere in the world. President Obama surprisingly inserted the word "rehabilitation" in his March 2011 directive on the future of Guantánamo ("Executive Order—Periodic Review of Individuals Detained at Guantánamo Bay Naval Station Pursuant to the Authorization for Use of Military Force"). Why not use this milestone moment in the war on terror to follow up in a concrete fashion?

Prosecuting Torture Tactics

4. *Revisit the issue of prosecuting those responsible for America's offshore torture policies in the Bush years:* The Obama administration made a decision not to investigate or prosecute the creators of the torture policy that defined the Bush administration's interrogation tactics in its war on terror. They did so, its officials claimed, in an effort to focus on the overwhelming issues the new presidency had to confront. They were visibly eager to avoid stoking a bitter partisan battle that they feared might further divide the country.

They banked instead on the idea that the lawyers and politicians responsible for that torture policy and the "black sites" and "extraordinary renditions" that went with it would quietly fade into the woodwork. This has obviously not been the case. On the contrary, in recent months former officials and members of the Bush administration have openly re-embraced those policies. In the aftermath of bin Laden's death, as if on cue, they immediately flooded the newspapers and airwaves with unsupportable claims that torture had led Washington to the al-Qaeda leader and should be a crucial part of the American arsenal in the future.

Forget for a moment that torture has still not been shown to have extracted valuable information (not otherwise available) from terror suspects. We know, in fact, that on a number of occasions it led investigators down the wrong path.

More importantly, it was a symptom of the war-on-terror frenzy that gripped this country and led it down the wrong path.

We now have all the proof we need that pretending torture never happened, legally speaking, only helps keep us embroiled in that "war" and the emotions it evokes. If the war on terror is ever to end, then tolerance for the support of torture has to end as well. Nothing would accomplish this better than the actual prosecution of the American crimes of that era—or at the very least, the investigation and official condemnation of those who sidestepped the Constitution and diminished the moral standing of the country at home and abroad.

Restoring Justice

5. Restore permanently to the Department of Justice responsibility for trying terrorists from around the globe: Since the fall of 2001, the Justice Department has been largely deprived of its portfolio for trying terrorists captured outside the United States. With the exception perhaps of cases involving terror attacks on military targets, there is no reason Justice should not prosecute such cases, as in the 1990s it successfully prosecuted the conspirators who first attacked the World Trade Center [in 1993], as it did in the African embassy bombings cases, and as it has recently done in Chicago in the case of Tahawwur Hussain Rana, who was convicted of providing material support to the terrorist group Lashkar-e-Taiba. (He was acquitted of conspiracy charges in the Mumbai bombing.) Since 9/11, the ability of judges, prosecutors, and defense attorneys to understand terrorism cases and try them responsibly has, if anything, increased immeasurably, while the military commissions system instituted by the Bush administration at Guantánamo and kept in place by President Obama has crashed disastrously and repeatedly on the shoals of politics, misinformation, and faulty procedure.

Whatever a commission might do when it came to bringing the war on terror officially to an end, this is the moment—with the death of bin Laden, the Arab uprisings, and the 10th anniversary of 9/11—to do it and to begin to seek ways to defend America even while guiding us back to our true self: a country with respect for the law, restraint when it comes to the use of force, and rights for all.

Periodical Bibliography

The following articles have been selected to supplement the diverse views presented in this chapter.

Ed Blanche	"US Attempts Annihilating Al Qaeda," *Middle East*, December 2011.
Dallas Boyd, Lewis A. Dunn, and James Scouras	"Why Has the United States Not Been Attacked Again?," *Washington Quarterly*, July 2009.
Jamie Dettmer, Christopher Dickey, and Eli Lake	"The Truth Behind the Benghazi Attack," *Newsweek*, October 29, 2012.
Thomas A. Devine	"At Home and Abroad: Restoring American Political Exceptionalism," *Harvard International Review*, Spring 2012.
Dennis Jett	"Losing the War on Terror: Who We Help Is Hurting," *Middle East Policy*, Fall 2012.
Joseph Lelyveld	"What 9/11 Wrought," *Smithsonian*, September 2011.
Paul Monk	"The Looming Reality of American Decline," *Quadrant*, July/August 2011.
Lauren B. O'Brien	"The Evolution of Terrorism Since 9/11," *FBI Law Enforcement Bulletin*, September 2011.
John L. Scherer	"Has Al Qaeda Been Beaten?," *USA Today Magazine*, September 2009.
Gabriel Schoenfeld	"In the Matter of George W. Bush v. the Constitution," *Commentary*, June 2008.
Jessica Stern	"Muslims in America," *National Interest*, May/June 2011.
Fareed Zakaria	"After Benghazi, Is al-Qaeda Back?," *Time*, October 15, 2012.

CHAPTER 4

What Principles Should Guide America's Conduct of War?

Chapter Preface

One facet of just war theory concerns the conduct of a nation and its troops during war. That is, a government and its armed forces are expected to act as humanely as possible in trying circumstances. This may include minimizing the suffering of civilians, treating captured combatants fairly, and otherwise acting justly in warfare (*jus in bello*) by not committing any internationally agreed upon war crimes. Many of these ethical codes are spelled out in the Geneva Conventions, articles of conduct signed by many nations at the conclusion of the Second World War. The agreements, however, do not cover all situations and contingencies, and the United States, a signatory of the Geneva Conventions, has been called to task in recent years for its actions during the war on terror.

Since 2004, two different US presidential administrations have stirred controversy for using unmanned drones to strike supposed terrorist targets inside neutral countries. Though the United States has not declared war on Pakistan, for example, more than 280 drone missiles have sought out concentrations of militants within its borders. Many more have pinpointed al Qaeda terrorist targets in Yemen. Brian Glyn Williams, a professor of Islamic history at the University of Massachusetts Dartmouth, argues that such strikes, which have a surgical precision that supposedly reduces or even eliminates the chance of civilian casualties, are looked upon favorably by locals in those countries. In an October 18, 2012, article for the *Guardian*, Williams is quoted as stating, "The drones are saving civilians, not killing them." Williams contends that civilians in areas hit by drones report that the militants are commonly killed or disrupted with little collateral damage. Bradley Jay Strawser, a former US Air Force officer and an assistant professor of philosophy at the Naval Postgraduate School, agrees. On July 14, 2012, the *New York Times* quoted Strawser as affirming, "All the evidence we have so far suggests that drones do better at both identifying the terrorist and avoiding collateral damage than anything else we have."

Outside the United States, the practice of drone warfare is not painted so optimistically. According to a June 13, 2012, Pew Research poll, more than half the populations in key European countries (France, Germany, Italy, and Spain, among others) disapprove of recent drone attacks on Pakistan, Yemen, and Somalia. In Arab nations such as Egypt, Tunisia, and Jordan, the portion of those opposed topped 70 percent. Perhaps explaining the resistance, the Pew report stated, "There remains a widespread perception that the U.S. acts unilaterally and does not consider the interests of other countries." Even in the United States, an opposition movement is growing. While the State Department has issued statements claiming the drone strikes were compliant with international codes of war and targeted only those people considered belligerents, Jonathan Manes of the American Civil Liberties Union told the Inter Press Service back in 2010, "We still don't know what criteria the government uses to determine that a civilian is acting like a fighter, and can therefore be killed, and . . . whether there are any geographical limits on where drone strikes can be used to target and kill individuals." The United Nations has begun a formal investigation into America's use of drones and their potential for killing innocents, and the administration of President Barack Obama has not closed off the possibility of aiding in that investigation.

The ethical nature of drone strikes is one prominent debate in America's conduct in the war on terror. In the following chapter, several authors consider other ethical questions regarding the country's pursuit of ending terrorism.

> *"Nuclear forces will continue to play an essential role in deterring potential adversaries, reassuring allies and partners around the world, and promoting stability globally and in key regions. But fundamental changes in the international security environment in recent years . . . enable us to fulfill those objectives at significantly lower nuclear force levels and with reduced reliance on nuclear weapons."*

America Must Reduce Its Nuclear Arsenal and Guarantee Limits on the Use of Nuclear Force

US Department of Defense

In the following viewpoint, the US Department of Defense (DOD)—which oversees America's conventional and nuclear forces and the nation's security—claims that since the end of the Cold War with the Soviet Union, the role of nuclear weapons in global politics and security has changed. Aligning its view with the rest of Barack Obama's presidential administration, the de-

US Department of Defense, "Nuclear Posture Review Report," April 2010.

partment asserts America's first concern should be to stop nuclear proliferation and ensure that no nuclear weapons end up in the hands of terrorists or other non-state actors. Beyond this, the DOD maintains that the United States must lead by example in making the world a safer place by drawing down its nuclear weapons in accordance with the New Strategic Arms Reduction Treaty. The department believes that because America and other nuclear powers have more missiles than needed to maintain deterrence, all parties can safely reduce their stockpiles. In addition, the DOD insists that in the post-Soviet era, nuclear weapons play a less vital role in American security. The department believes the nation's conventional forces have and will continue to play a more central role in backing up American foreign policy, thus making a large nuclear force unnecessary.

As you read, consider the following questions:

1. According to the Department of Defense, by what percentage have the United States and Russia reduced their deployed nuclear weapons since the end of the Cold War?

2. What is the advantage of the stockpile management program, as the DOD outlines it?

3. What is "negative security assurance," as the DOD explains?

The international security environment has changed dramatically since the end of the Cold War [a period of tension between the United States and the Soviet Union during the second half of the twentieth century]. The threat of global nuclear war has become remote, but the risk of nuclear attack has increased.

The Threat of Nuclear Proliferation and Nuclear Terrorism

The most immediate and extreme threat today is nuclear terrorism. Al Qaeda and their extremist allies are seeking nuclear weapons. We must assume they would use such weapons if they managed to obtain them. Although terrorist groups are currently believed to lack the resources to produce weapons-usable nuclear material themselves, the vulnerability to theft or seizure of vast stocks of such nuclear materials around the world, and the availability of sensitive equipment and technologies in the nuclear black market, create a serious risk that terrorists may acquire what they need to build a nuclear weapon.

To date, the international community has made progress toward achieving a global "lock down" of nuclear weapons, materials, and associated technology, but much more work needs to be done. In addition, the United States and the international community have improving but currently insufficient capabilities to detect, interdict, and defeat efforts to covertly deliver nuclear materials or weapons—and if an attack occurs, to respond to minimize casualties and economic impact as well as to attribute the source of the attack and take strong action.

Today's other pressing threat is nuclear proliferation. Additional countries—especially those at odds with the United States, its allies and partners, and the broader international community—may acquire nuclear weapons. In pursuit of their nuclear ambitions, North Korea and Iran have violated non-proliferation obligations, defied directives of the United Nations Security Council, pursued missile delivery capabilities, and resisted international efforts to resolve through diplomatic means the crises they have created. Their illicit supply of arms and sensitive material and technologies has heightened global proliferation risks and regional tensions. Their provocative behavior has increased instability in their regions. Continued noncompliance with nonproliferation norms by these and other countries would seriously weaken the Nuclear Non-Proliferation Treaty (NPT) [officially known as the Treaty on the Non-Proliferation of Nuclear Weapons], with adverse security implications for the United States and the international community at large.

The potential for regional aggression by these states raises challenges not only of deterrence, but also of reassuring U.S. allies and partners. In the Cold War, our allies sought assurance that they would remain safe in the face of Soviet threats because the United States was demonstrably committed to their security. Today's environment is quite different. Some U.S. allies are increasingly anxious about changes in the security environment, including nuclear and missile proliferation, and desire reassurance that the United States will remain committed to their security. A failure of reassurance could lead to a decision by one or more nonnuclear states to seek nuclear deterrents of their own, an outcome which could contribute to an unraveling of the NPT regime and to a greater likelihood of nuclear weapon use.

Despite these challenges, the NPT remains a cornerstone of the nonproliferation regime and has served the international community well over the past four decades. Its fundamental bargain is still sound: all parties have a right to peaceful nuclear power; states without nuclear weapons forsake them; and those with nuclear weapons work toward disarmament. . . .

Strategic Stability with Russia and China

While facing the urgent threats of nuclear terrorism and nuclear proliferation, the United States must continue to address the more familiar challenge of ensuring strategic stability with existing nuclear powers—most notably Russia and China. Russia remains America's only peer in the area of nuclear weapons capabilities. But the nature of the U.S.-Russia strategic and political relationship has changed fundamentally since the days of the Cold War. Policy differences continue to arise between the two countries, and Russia continues to modernize its still-formidable nuclear forces. But Russia and the United States have increased their cooperation in areas of shared interest, including preventing nuclear proliferation and nuclear terrorism. And the prospects for military confrontation have declined dramatically in recent decades.

While the United States and Russia have reduced deployed nuclear weapons by about 75 percent since the end of the Cold War, each still retains more nuclear weapons than necessary for stable deterrence. As the United States and Russia reduce their deployed strategic nuclear weapons and delivery vehicles under the New Strategic Arms Reduction Treaty (New START) and a follow-on agreement to it, maintaining a stable bilateral balance and avoiding dangerous nuclear competition will be key objectives.

The United States and China are increasingly interdependent and their shared responsibilities for addressing global security threats, such as WMD [weapons of mass destruction] proliferation and terrorism, are growing. The United States welcomes a strong, prosperous, and successful China that plays a greater global role in supporting international rules, norms, and institutions.

At the same time, the United States and China's Asian neighbors remain concerned about the pace and scope of China's current military modernization efforts, including its quantitative and qualitative modernization of its nuclear capabilities. China's nuclear arsenal remains much smaller than the arsenals of Russia and the United States. But the lack of transparency surrounding its programs—their pace and scope as well as the strategy and doctrine guiding them—raises questions about China's future strategic intentions. . . .

Reduced Nuclear Force Levels Still Guarantee Deterrence

The massive nuclear arsenal we inherited from the Cold War era of bipolar military confrontation is poorly suited to address the challenges posed by suicidal terrorists and unfriendly regimes seeking nuclear weapons. Therefore, it is essential that we better align our nuclear policies and posture to our most urgent priorities—preventing nuclear terrorism and nuclear proliferation.

This does not mean that our nuclear deterrent has become irrelevant. Indeed, as long as nuclear weapons exist, the United States will maintain safe, secure, and effective nuclear forces, including deployed and stockpiled nuclear weapons, highly capable nuclear delivery systems and command and control capabilities, and the physical infrastructure and the expert personnel needed to sustain them. These nuclear forces will continue to play an essential role in deterring potential adversaries, reassuring allies and partners around the world, and promoting stability globally and in key regions.

But fundamental changes in the international security environment in recent years—including the growth of unrivaled U.S. conventional military capabilities, major improvements in missile defenses, and the easing of Cold War rivalries—enable us to fulfill those objectives at significantly lower nuclear force levels and with reduced reliance on nuclear weapons. Therefore, without jeopardizing our traditional deterrence and reassurance goals, we are now able to shape our nuclear weapons policies and force structure in ways that will better enable us to meet today's most pressing security challenges.

- By reducing the role and numbers of U.S. nuclear weapons—and thereby demonstrating that we are meeting our NPT Article VI obligation to make progress toward nuclear disarmament—we can put ourselves in a much stronger position to persuade our NPT partners to join with us in adopting the measures needed to reinvigorate the nonproliferation regime and secure nuclear materials worldwide against theft or seizure by terrorist groups.

- By maintaining a credible nuclear deterrent and reinforcing regional security architectures with missile defenses and other conventional military capabilities, we can reassure our nonnuclear allies and partners worldwide of our security commitments to them and confirm that they do not need nuclear weapons capabilities of their own.

- By pursuing a sound stockpile management program for extending the life of U.S. nuclear weapons, we can ensure a safe, secure, and effective deterrent without the development of new nuclear warheads or further nuclear testing.

- By modernizing our aging nuclear weapons–supporting facilities and investing in human capital, we can substantially reduce the number of stockpiled nuclear weapons we retain as a hedge against technical or geopolitical surprise, accelerate the dismantlement of nuclear weapons no longer required for our deterrent, and improve our understanding of foreign nuclear weapons activities.

- By promoting strategic stability with Russia and China and improving transparency and mutual confidence, we can help create the conditions for moving toward a world without nuclear weapons and build a stronger basis for addressing the threats of nuclear proliferation and nuclear terrorism.

- By working to reduce the salience of nuclear weapons in international affairs and moving step-by-step toward eliminating them, we can reverse the growing expectation that we are destined to live in a world with many nuclear-armed states, and decrease incentives for additional countries to hedge against an uncertain and dan-

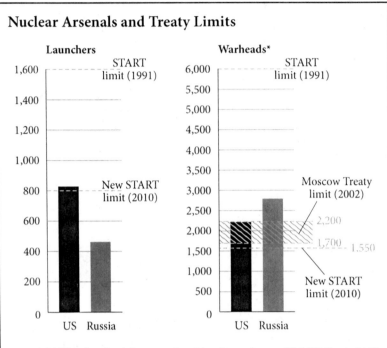

Nuclear Arsenals and Treaty Limits

Launchers

Warheads*

START limit (1991)

New START limit (2010)

Moscow Treaty limit (2002)

2,200

1,700   1,550

New START limit (2010)

US   Russia

US   Russia

* Additional warheads in reserve / awaiting dismantlement: US 6,700, Russia 8,150

TAKEN FROM: Bulletin of the Atomic Scientists in BBC News, "US and Russia Announce Deal to Cut Nuclear Weapons," March 26, 2010. http://news.bbc.co.uk.

gerous future by pursuing nuclear options of their own. Creating these conditions will reduce the likelihood of nuclear weapon use.

In sum, the security environment has changed in fundamental ways since the end of the Cold War. The landscape of threats and challenges has evolved. But a changing landscape has also brought with it some valuable new opportunities. Accordingly, U.S. policy priorities must shift. The U.S. policy agenda must reflect a clear and current understanding of how U.S. nuclear strategy and posture shape these international dynamics. . . .

Reducing the Role of U.S. Nuclear Weapons

The role of nuclear weapons in U.S. national security and U.S. military strategy has been reduced significantly in recent decades, but further steps can and should be taken at this time.

The fundamental role of U.S. nuclear weapons, which will continue as long as nuclear weapons exist, is to deter nuclear attack on the United States, our allies, and partners.

During the Cold War, the United States also reserved the right to use nuclear weapons in response to a massive conventional attack by the Soviet Union and its Warsaw Pact allies. Moreover, after the United States gave up its own chemical and biological weapons (CBW) pursuant to international treaties (while some states continued to possess or pursue them) the United States reserved the right to employ nuclear weapons to deter CBW attack on the United States and its allies and partners.

Since the end of the Cold War, the strategic situation has changed in fundamental ways.

First, and foremost, the Soviet Union and the Warsaw Pact are gone. Russia is not an enemy, and is increasingly a partner in confronting proliferation and other emerging threats. And all of the non-Soviet former members of the Warsaw Pact are now members of the North Atlantic Treaty Organization (NATO).

Second, U.S., allied, and partner conventional military capabilities now provide a wide range of effective conventional response options to deter and if necessary defeat conventional threats from regional actors. Major improvements in missile defenses and counter–weapons of mass destruction (WMD) capabilities have strengthened deterrence and defense against CBW attack.

Given these developments, the role of U.S. nuclear weapons to deter and respond to nonnuclear attacks—conventional, biological, or chemical—has declined significantly. The

United States will continue to reduce the role of nuclear weapons in deterring nonnuclear attack.

To that end, the United States is now prepared to strengthen its long-standing "negative security assurance" by declaring that the United States will not use or threaten to use nuclear weapons against nonnuclear weapons states that are party to the Nuclear Non-Proliferation Treaty (NPT) and in compliance with their nuclear nonproliferation obligations.

This revised assurance is intended to underscore the security benefits of adhering to and fully complying with the NPT and persuade nonnuclear weapon states party to the treaty to work with the United States and other interested parties to adopt effective measures to strengthen the nonproliferation regime.

> *"With less than 2 percent of the defense budget at stake in the nuclear forces, drastic, ideologically driven cuts now . . . could end up being one of history's most expensive 'cheap thrills.'"*

America Should Not Reduce Its Nuclear Arsenal

G. Philip Hughes

In the following viewpoint, G. Philip Hughes questions President Barack Obama's objective of reducing US nuclear forces below those demanded by international treaty. Hughes claims Obama is hoping to present himself as a man of peace, but Hughes fears the posturing overshadows the serious consequences of cutting America's nuclear capabilities. Hughes contends that a weakened nuclear arsenal may not seem a deterrent to antagonistic nations on the path toward achieving nuclear weapons status. Additionally, Hughes argues that a smaller nuclear force might make a vulnerable target for nations seeking a nuclear first strike. A former ambassador and White House national security aide for presidents Ronald Reagan and George H.W. Bush, G. Philip Hughes now serves as senior director of the White House Writers Group, a policy communications firm.

As you read, consider the following questions:

1. According to Hughes, reports in May 2012 suggested the Obama administration may be considering cutting US nuclear warheads to what number?

2. Why does Hughes contend that China's nuclear arsenal might be larger than reported?

3. According to the author, roughly how many allied nations are protected by America's nuclear defense capabilities?

Have you noticed how much of what passes for political leadership today amounts to easy, simple, intuitively popular gestures? The idea is to collect an immediate political benefit while obscuring and discounting the long-term costs.

That's a reasonable summary of the [Barack] Obama administration's approach to U.S. national security where nuclear deterrence is concerned. With the Cold War [a period of tension between the United States and the Soviet Union during the second half of the twentieth century] now more than two decades behind us, the U.S.-Soviet nuclear standoff that was its centerpiece seems obviously anachronistic today. Despite the [Vladimir] Putin/[Dmitry] Medvedev regime's crude nationalism and politically opportunistic anti-U.S. rhetoric, few can imagine plausible scenarios for a U.S.-Russian nuclear confrontation. Similarly, despite the vague, prevalent sense that China's spectacular economic rise will portend geopolitical rivalry, and possible conflict, with the United States, few imagine convincing circumstances for a nuclear confrontation, save some future, stunningly miscalculated brinksmanship over Taiwan.

A Dangerous Drawdown

Of the other nuclear powers, Britain, France, and Israel are our allies, and India's and Pakistan's arsenals are geared to their mutual nuclear standoff. As to today's upstart nuclear proliferators—North Korea and Iran—it is widely assumed that the U.S. nuclear deterrent would so overmatch whatever nascent nuclear capabilities they might develop that U.S. forces would be unquestionably adequate to deter any threats against us or our allies. And then there are the anxious-making scenarios of terrorists acquiring one or a few nuclear weapons, presumably from a destabilized Pakistan or a malignant Iran, for use against the United States. But few can suggest plausible ways that the sizeable U.S. nuclear arsenal would come directly into play deterring this menace.

All of which has set up an environment in which it's been safe for President Obama to embrace the ultimate goal of eliminating nuclear weapons from the world, as he did in Prague in 2009. And it incentivizes him to push for further radical nuclear reductions with Russia, beyond the New START [New Strategic Arms Reduction Treaty] limits of 1,550 operational nuclear weapons and 800 strategic launchers agreed just two years ago this month [April 2012]. Reports last month indicated that Obama's team was considering reducing U.S. operational nuclear weapons to as few as 300–400 warheads—placing the nuclear arsenal of the world's supposed "sole remaining superpower" on par with those of Britain, France, or . . . ahem . . . Pakistan! Or, for that matter, of China—although recent reports of a 3,000-mile network of Chinese tunnels concealing its nuclear weapons activities suggest that we might know less than we imagine about China's actual nuclear capabilities.

In pursuing these cuts, Obama is pushing on an open door. To a public unconcerned about issues of nuclear deterrence, Obama looks virtuous—a man of peace. For his own party, particularly its antinuclear left-wing, he's able to deliver, seemingly costlessly, on their most fervent hopes for nuclear disarmament—especially U.S. nuclear disarmament. Having failed to satisfy many of their other fervent hopes—"card check" for unions, tax hikes on the rich, closing Guantánamo [referring to the detention facility for prisoners of the wars in Afghanistan and Iraq], etc.—giving up "more nuclear weapons than we need" via arms agreements with Russia is an obvious "cheap thrill" for his base. And Republican opposition will be limited. With the imminent retirement of Sen. Jon Kyl, few in Congress enjoy deep expertise on nuclear deterrence and arms control issues. And, in any case, arguing for more—not fewer—U.S. nuclear weapons in an election-year environment is an obvious political loser.

Unknowns That Might Jeopardize Security

So, what's the problem? Just this. Obama's nuclear weapons policies are based on nothing more than a collection of untested assumptions. What if they're wrong?

- How do we know that a greatly reduced deterrent force, even if roughly equivalent to Russia's, will be adequate to deter all other comers in a proliferated world with a nuclear North Korea and/or Iran?

- How do we know that a minimal deterrent force, à la France, would be adequate to extend deterrence to the 30-plus allies currently defended by the U.S. nuclear arsenal—and so dissuade them from pursuing their own nuclear capabilities?

- How do we know that a "superpower" with an arsenal of a few hundred operational warheads wouldn't merely tempt other nascent nuclear powers to reach or surpass that level—something within reach—becoming modern-day "mice that roared"?

- If deep nuclear reductions make maintaining three independent legs of the nuclear triad—land- and submarine-based missiles and bombers—uneconomical, how do we know that we will not have introduced a fatal vulnerability into our deterrent force, permitting it to be crippled or neutralized by even a small nation's nuclear attack?

- Indeed, how do we know that a very small U.S. deterrent force—a weigh station on the road to Obama's "zero nukes" goal—won't actually destabilize deterrence, tempting an aggressor with an appreciable chance of a successful disarming first strike?

Politically attractive as his nuclear reductions agenda seems, even President Obama, posturing as the "man of peace" meriting his Nobel Peace Prize, must be able to see the irony here. With less than 2 percent of the defense budget at stake in the nuclear forces, drastic, ideologically driven cuts now that heighten the risks of future nuclear conflict, and the uncertainty of the outcome, could end up being one of history's most expensive "cheap thrills."

"Torture is not always impermissible. However rare the cases, there are circumstances in which, by any rational moral calculus, torture not only would be permissible but would be required."

America Is Justified in Utilizing Torture to Pursue Terrorists

Charles Krauthammer

Charles Krauthammer is a Pulitzer Prize–winning columnist and a contributing editor for the Weekly Standard, *a conservative newsmagazine. In the following viewpoint, Krauthammer argues against the passing of the Detainee Treatment Act in December 2005. This act, proposed by Senator John McCain, prevents US military or security agents from inflicting cruel or inhumane punishment on prisoners. Krauthammer believes that while the motivation for the legislation may be just, there are instances in which American lives or national security may depend on the torture of terrorists or other persons acting outside the codes of legitimate war. In such cases, Krauthammer maintains that torture should be acceptable under strict guidelines and oversight.*

Charles Krauthammer, "The Truth About Torture," *Weekly Standard*, vol. 11, no. 12, December 5, 2005. Copyright © 2005 by Charles Krauthammer. All rights reserved. Reproduced by permission.

As you read, consider the following questions:

1. Why, if terrorists are entitled to no protections under military law, does the United States treat captured terrorists humanely, according to Krauthammer?

2. What events does Krauthammer imply caused Israel to change its laws regarding the "physical coercion" of prisoners?

3. In Krauthammer's hypothetical model of an America that permitted forceful coercion in limited cases, from whom must specialized interrogation agents acquire authorization to use torture?

During the last few weeks in Washington the pieties about torture have lain so thick in the air that it has been impossible to have a reasoned discussion. The McCain amendment that would ban "cruel, inhuman, or degrading" treatment of any prisoner by any agent of the United States sailed through the Senate by a vote of 90-9. The Washington establishment remains stunned that nine such retrograde, morally inert persons—let alone senators—could be found in this noble capital.

Now, John McCain has great moral authority on this issue, having heroically borne torture at the hands of the North Vietnamese. McCain has made fine arguments in defense of his position. And McCain is acting out of the deep and honorable conviction that what he is proposing is not only right but is in the best interest of the United States. His position deserves respect. But that does not mean, as seems to be the assumption in Washington today, that a critical analysis of his "no torture, ever" policy is beyond the pale.

Let's begin with a few analytic distinctions. For the purpose of torture and prisoner maltreatment, there are three kinds of war prisoners:

First, there is the ordinary soldier caught on the field of battle. There is no question that he is entitled to humane treatment. Indeed, we have no right to disturb a hair on his head. His detention has but a single purpose: to keep him *hors de combat*. The proof of that proposition is that if there were a better way to keep him off the battlefield that did not require his detention, we would let him go. Indeed, during one year of the Civil War, the two sides did try an alternative. They mutually "paroled" captured enemy soldiers, i.e., released them to return home on the pledge that they would not take up arms again. (The experiment failed for a foreseeable reason: cheating. Grant found that some paroled Confederates had reenlisted.)

Because the only purpose of detention in these circumstances is to prevent the prisoner from becoming a combatant again, he is entitled to all the protections and dignity of an ordinary domestic prisoner—indeed, more privileges, because, unlike the domestic prisoner, he has committed no crime. He merely had the misfortune to enlist on the other side of a legitimate war. He is therefore entitled to many of the privileges enjoyed by an ordinary citizen—the right to send correspondence, to engage in athletic activity and intellectual pursuits, to receive allowances from relatives—except, of course, for the freedom to leave the prison.

Second, there is the captured terrorist. A terrorist is by profession, indeed by definition, an unlawful combatant: He lives outside the laws of war because he does not wear a uniform, he hides among civilians, and he deliberately targets innocents. He is entitled to no protections whatsoever. People seem to think that the postwar Geneva Conventions were written only to protect detainees. In fact, their deeper purpose was to provide a deterrent to the kind of barbaric treatment of civilians that had become so horribly apparent during the first half of the 20th century, and in particular, during the Second World War. The idea was to deter the abuse of civilians by promising combatants who treated noncombatants well that they themselves would be treated according to a code of dignity if captured—and, crucially, that they would be denied the protections of that code if they broke the laws of war and abused civilians themselves.

Breaking the laws of war and abusing civilians are what, to understate the matter vastly, terrorists do for a living. They are entitled, therefore, to nothing. Anyone who blows up a car bomb in a market deserves to spend the rest of his life roasting on a spit over an open fire. But we don't do that because we do not descend to the level of our enemy. We don't do that because, unlike him, we are civilized. Even though terrorists are entitled to no humane treatment, we give it to them because it is in our nature as a moral and humane people. And when on rare occasions we fail to do that, as has occurred in several of the fronts of the war on terror, we are duly disgraced.

The norm, however, is how the majority of prisoners at Guantánamo have been treated. We give them three meals a day, superior medical care, and provision to pray five times a day. Our scrupulousness extends even to providing them with their own Korans, which is the only reason alleged abuses of the Koran at Guantánamo ever became an issue. That we should have provided those who kill innocents in the name of Islam with precisely the document that inspires their barbarism is a sign of the absurd lengths to which we often go in extending undeserved humanity to terrorist prisoners.

Third, there is the terrorist with information. Here the issue of torture gets complicated and the easy pieties don't so easily apply. Let's take the textbook case. Ethics 101: A terrorist has planted a nuclear bomb in New York City. It will go off in one hour. A million people will die. You capture the terrorist. He knows where it is. He's not talking.

Question: If you have the slightest belief that hanging this man by his thumbs will get you the information to save a million people, are you permitted to do it?

Now, on most issues regarding torture, I confess tentativeness and uncertainty. But on this issue, there can be no uncertainty: Not only is it permissible to hang this miscreant by his thumbs. It is a moral duty.

Yes, you say, but that's an extreme and very hypothetical case. Well, not as hypothetical as you think. Sure, the (nuclear) scale is hypothetical, but in the age of the car and suicide bomber, terrorists are often captured who have just set a car bomb to go off or sent a suicide bomber out to a coffee shop, and you only have minutes to find out where the attack is to take place. This "hypothetical" is common enough that the Israelis have a term for precisely that situation: the ticking time bomb problem.

And even if the example I gave were entirely hypothetical, the conclusion—yes, in this case even torture is permissible—is telling because it establishes the principle: Torture is not always impermissible. However rare the cases, there are circumstances in which, by any rational moral calculus, torture not only would be permissible but would be required (to acquire lifesaving information). And once you've established the principle, to paraphrase George Bernard Shaw, all that's left to haggle about is the price. In the case of torture, that means that the argument is not whether torture is ever permissible, but when—i.e., under what obviously stringent circumstances: how big, how imminent, how preventable the ticking time bomb.

That is why the McCain amendment, which by mandating "torture never" refuses even to recognize the legitimacy of any moral calculus, cannot be right. There must be exceptions. The real argument should be over what constitutes a legitimate exception.

Let's take an example that is far from hypothetical. You capture Khalid Sheikh Mohammed in Pakistan. He not only has already killed innocents, he is deeply involved in the planning for the present and future killing of innocents. He not only was the architect of the 9/11 attack that killed nearly three thousand people in one day, most of them dying a terrible, agonizing, indeed tortured death. But as the top al Qaeda planner and logistical expert, he also knows a lot about terror attacks to come. He knows plans, identities, contacts, materials, cell locations, safe houses, cased targets, etc. What do you do with him?

We have recently learned that since 9/11 the United States has maintained a series of "black sites" around the world, secret detention centers where presumably high-level terrorists like Khalid Sheikh Mohammed have been imprisoned. The world is scandalized. Black sites? Secret detention? Jimmy Carter calls this "a profound and radical change in the . . . moral values of our country." The Council of Europe demands an investigation, calling the claims "extremely worrying." Its human rights commissioner declares "such practices" to constitute "a serious human rights violation, and further proof of the crisis of values" that has engulfed the war on terror. The gnashing of teeth and rending of garments has been considerable.

I myself have not gnashed a single tooth. My garments remain entirely unrent. Indeed, I feel reassured. It would be a gross dereliction of duty for any government not to keep Khalid Sheikh Mohammed isolated, disoriented, alone, despairing, cold and sleepless, in some godforsaken hidden location in order to find out what he knew about plans for future mass murder. What are we supposed to do? Give him a nice cell in a warm Manhattan prison, complete with *Miranda* rights, a mellifluent lawyer, and his own website? Are not those the kinds of courtesies we extended to the 1993 World Trade Center bombers, then congratulated ourselves on how we "brought to justice" those responsible for an attack that barely failed to kill tens of thousands of Americans, only to discover a decade later that we had accomplished nothing—indeed, that some of the disclosures at the trial had helped Osama bin Laden avoid U.S. surveillance?

Have we learned nothing from 9/11? Are we prepared to go back with complete amnesia to the domestic-crime model of dealing with terrorists, which allowed us to sleepwalk through the nineties while al Qaeda incubated and grew and metastasized unmolested until on 9/11 it finished what the first World Trade Center bombers had begun?

Let's assume (and hope) that Khalid Sheikh Mohammed has been kept in one of these black sites, say, a cell somewhere in Romania, held entirely incommunicado and subjected to the kind of "coercive interrogation" that I described above. McCain has been going around praising the Israelis as the model of how to deal with terrorism and prevent terrorist attacks. He does so because in 1999 the Israeli Supreme Court outlawed all torture in the course of interrogation. But in reality, the Israeli case is far more complicated. And the complications reflect precisely the dilemmas regarding all coercive interrogation, the weighing of the lesser of two evils: the undeniable inhumanity of torture versus the abdication of the duty to protect the victims of a potentially preventable mass murder.

In a summary of Israel's policies, Glenn Frankel of the *Washington Post* noted that the 1999 Supreme Court ruling struck down secret guidelines established 12 years earlier that allowed interrogators to use the kind of physical and psychological pressure I described in imagining how KSM [Khalid Sheikh Mohammed] might be treated in America's "black sites."

"But after the second Palestinian uprising broke out a year later, and especially after a devastating series of suicide bombings of passenger buses, cafes and other civilian targets," writes

Frankel, citing human rights lawyers and detainees, "Israel's internal security service, known as the Shin Bet or the Shabak, returned to physical coercion as a standard practice." Not only do the techniques used "command widespread support from the Israeli public," but "Israeli prime ministers and justice ministers with a variety of political views," including the most conciliatory and liberal, have defended these techniques "as a last resort in preventing terrorist attacks."

Which makes McCain's position on torture incoherent. If this kind of coercive interrogation were imposed on any inmate in the American prison system, it would immediately be declared cruel and unusual, and outlawed. How can he oppose these practices, which the Israelis use, and yet hold up Israel as a model for dealing with terrorists? Or does he countenance this kind of interrogation in extreme circumstances—in which case, what is left of his categorical opposition to inhuman treatment of any kind?

But let us push further into even more unpleasant territory, the territory that lies beyond mere coercive interrogation and beyond McCain's self-contradictions. How far are we willing to go?

This "going beyond" need not be cinematic and ghoulish. (Jay Leno once suggested "duct tape" for Khalid Sheikh Mohammed.) Consider, for example, injection with Sodium Pentothal. (Colloquially known as "truth serum," it is nothing of the sort. It is a barbiturate whose purpose is to sedate. Its effects are much like that of alcohol: disinhibiting the higher brain centers to make someone more likely to disclose information or thoughts that might otherwise be guarded.) Forcible sedation is a clear violation of bodily integrity. In a civilian context it would be considered assault. It is certainly impermissible under any prohibition of cruel, inhuman, or degrading treatment.

Let's posit that during the interrogation of Khalid Sheikh Mohammed, perhaps early on, we got intelligence about an imminent al Qaeda attack. And we had a very good reason to believe he knew about it. And if we knew what he knew, we could stop it. If we thought we could glean a critical piece of information by use of Sodium Pentothal, would we be permitted to do so?

Less hypothetical, there is waterboarding, a terrifying and deeply shocking torture technique in which the prisoner has his face exposed to water in a way that gives the feeling of drowning. According to CIA sources cited by ABC News, Khalid Sheikh Mohammed "was able to last between two and 2 1/2 minutes before begging to confess." Should we regret having done that? Should we abolish by law that practice, so that it could never be used on the next Khalid Sheikh Mohammed having thus gotten his confession?

And what if he possessed information with less imminent implications? Say we had information about a cell that he had helped found or direct, and that cell was planning some major attack and we needed information about the identity and location of its members. A rational moral calculus might not permit measures as extreme as the nuke-in-Manhattan scenario, but would surely permit measures beyond mere psychological pressure.

Such a determination would not be made with an untroubled conscience. It would be troubled because there is no denying the monstrous evil that is any form of torture. And there is no denying how corrupting it can be to the individuals and society that practice it. But elected leaders, responsible above all for the protection of their citizens, have the obligation to tolerate their own sleepless nights by doing what is necessary—and only what is necessary, nothing more—to get information that could prevent mass murder.

Given the gravity of the decision, if we indeed cross the Rubicon—as we must—we need rules. The problem with the McCain amendment is that once you have gone public with a

Little Change in Americans' Opinions about Torture of Suspected Terrorists

Torture to gain important information from suspected terrorists is justified...	Nov 2007	Feb 2008	Feb 2009	Apr 2009
Often	18%	17%	16%	15%
Sometimes	30%	31%	28%	34%
Rarely	21%	20%	20%	22%
Never	27%	30%	31%	25%
Don't know	4%	2%	5%	4%
Often/Sometimes	48%	48%	44%	49%
Rarely/Never	48%	50%	51%	47%

TAKEN FROM: Pew Research Center, "Public Remains Divided Over Use of Torture," April 24, 2009.

blanket ban on all forms of coercion, it is going to be very difficult to publicly carve out exceptions. The Bush administration is to be faulted for having attempted such a codification with the kind of secrecy, lack of coherence, and lack of strict enforcement that led us to the McCain reaction.

What to do at this late date? Begin, as McCain does, by banning all forms of coercion or inhuman treatment by anyone serving in the military—an absolute ban on torture by all military personnel everywhere. We do not want a private somewhere making these fine distinctions about ticking and slow-fuse time bombs. We don't even want colonels or generals making them. It would be best for the morale, discipline, and honor of the armed forces for the United States to maintain an absolute prohibition, both to simplify their task in making decisions and to offer them whatever reciprocal treatment they might receive from those who capture them— although I have no illusion that any anti-torture provision will soften the heart of a single jihadist holding a knife to the throat of a captured American soldier. We would impose this restriction on ourselves for our own reasons of military discipline and military honor.

Outside the military, however, I would propose, contra McCain, a ban against all forms of torture, coercive interrogation, and inhuman treatment, except in two contingencies: (1) the ticking time bomb and (2) the slower-fuse high-level terrorist (such as KSM). Each contingency would have its own set of rules. In the case of the ticking time bomb, the rules would be relatively simple: Nothing rationally related to getting accurate information would be ruled out. The case of the high-value suspect with slow-fuse information is more complicated. The principle would be that the level of inhumanity of the measures used (moral honesty is essential here—we would be using measures that are by definition inhumane) would be proportional to the need and value of the information. Interrogators would be constrained to use the least inhumane treatment necessary relative to the magnitude and imminence of the evil being prevented and the importance of the knowledge being obtained.

These exceptions to the no-torture rule would not be granted to just any nonmilitary interrogators, or anyone with CIA credentials. They would be reserved for highly specialized agents who are experts and experienced in interrogation. . . . Nor would they be acting on their own. They would be required to obtain written permission for such interrogations from the highest political authorities in the country (cabinet level) or from a quasi-judicial body modeled on the Foreign Intelligence Surveillance Court (which permits what would ordinarily be illegal searches and seizures in the war on terror). Or, if the bomb was truly ticking and there was no time, the interrogators would be allowed to act on their own, but would require post facto authorization within, say, 24 hours of their interrogation, so that they knew that whatever they did would be subject to review by others and be justified only under the most stringent terms.

One of the purposes of these justifications would be to establish that whatever extreme measures are used are for reasons of nothing but information. Historically, the torture of prisoners has been done for a variety of reasons apart from information, most prominently reasons of justice or revenge. We do not do that. We should not do that. Ever. Khalid Sheikh Mohammed, murderer of 2,973 innocents, is surely deserving of the most extreme suffering day and night for the rest of his life. But it is neither our role nor our right to be the agents of that suffering. Vengeance is mine, sayeth the Lord. His, not ours. Torture is a terrible and monstrous thing, as degrading and morally corrupting to those who practice it as any conceivable human activity including its moral twin, capital punishment.

If Khalid Sheikh Mohammed knew nothing, or if we had reached the point where his knowledge had been exhausted, I'd be perfectly prepared to throw him into a nice, comfortable Manhattan cell and give him a trial to determine what would be fit and just punishment. But as long as he had useful information, things would be different.

Very different. And it simply will not do to take refuge in the claim that all of the above discussion is superfluous because torture never works anyway. Would that this were true. Unfortunately, on its face, this is nonsense. Is one to believe that in the entire history of human warfare, no combatant has ever received useful information by the use of pressure, torture, or any other kind of inhuman treatment? It may indeed be true that torture is not a reliable tool. But that is very different from saying that it is never useful.

The monstrous thing about torture is that sometimes it does work. In 1994, 19-year-old Israeli corporal Nachshon Wachsman was kidnapped by Palestinian terrorists. The Israelis captured the driver of the car used in the kidnapping and tortured him in order to find where Wachsman was being held. Yitzhak Rabin, prime minister and peacemaker, admitted that they tortured him in a way that went even beyond the '87 guidelines for "coercive interrogation" later struck down by the Israeli Supreme Court as too harsh. The driver talked. His information was accurate. The Israelis found Wachsman. "If we'd been so careful to follow the ['87] Landau Commission [which allowed coercive interrogation]," explained Rabin, "we would never have found out where Wachsman was being held."

In the Wachsman case, I would have done precisely what Rabin did. (The fact that Wachsman's Palestinian captors killed him during the Israeli rescue raid makes the case doubly tragic, but changes nothing of the moral calculus.) Faced with a similar choice, an American president would have a similar obligation. To do otherwise—to give up the chance to find your soldier lest you sully yourself by authorizing torture of the person who possesses potentially lifesaving information—is a deeply immoral betrayal of a soldier and countryman. Not as cosmically immoral as permitting a city of one's countrymen to perish, as in the Ethics 101 case. But it remains, nonetheless, a case of moral abdication—of a kind rather parallel to that of the principled pacifist. There is much to admire in those who refuse on principle ever to take up arms under any conditions. But that does not make pure pacifism, like no-torture absolutism, any less a form of moral foolishness, tinged with moral vanity. Not reprehensible, only deeply reproachable and supremely impracticable. People who hold such beliefs are deserving of a certain respect. But they are not to be put in positions of authority. One should be grateful for the saintly among us. And one should be vigilant that they not get to make the decisions upon which the lives of others depend.

Which brings us to the greatest irony of all in the torture debate. I have just made what will be characterized as the pro-torture case contra McCain by proposing two major exceptions carved out of any no-torture rule: the ticking time bomb and the slow-fuse high-value terrorist. McCain supposedly is being hailed for defending all that is good and right and just in America by standing foursquare against any inhuman treatment. Or is he?

According to *Newsweek*, in the ticking time bomb case McCain says that the president should disobey the very law that McCain seeks to pass—under the justification that "you do what you have to do. But you take responsibility for it." But if torturing the ticking time bomb suspect is "what you have to do," then why has McCain been going around arguing that such things must never be done?

As for exception number two, the high-level terrorist with slow-fuse information, Stuart Taylor, the superb legal correspondent for *National Journal*, argues that with appropriate legal interpretation, the "cruel, inhuman, or degrading" standard, "though vague, is said by experts to codify . . . the commonsense principle that the toughness of interrogation techniques should be calibrated to the importance and urgency of the information likely to be obtained." That would permit "some very aggressive techniques . . . on that small percentage of detainees who seem especially likely to have potentially lifesaving information." Or as Evan Thomas and Michael Hirsh put it in the *Newsweek* report on McCain and torture, the McCain standard would "presumably allow for a sliding scale" of torture or torture-lite or other coercive techniques, thus permitting "for a very small percentage—those High Value Targets like Khalid Sheikh Mohammed—some pretty rough treatment."

But if that is the case, then McCain embraces the same exceptions I do, but prefers to pretend he does not. If that is the case, then his much-touted and endlessly repeated absolutism on inhumane treatment is merely for show. If that is the case, then the moral preening and the phony arguments can stop now, and we can all agree that in this real world of astonishingly murderous enemies, in two very circumscribed circumstances, we must all be prepared to torture. Having established that, we can then begin to work together to codify rules of interrogation for the two very unpleasant but very real cases in which we are morally permitted—indeed morally compelled—to do terrible things.

| "*If torture is not wrong, nothing is wrong.*"

Torture Is Never Justified

Jamie Mayerfeld

In the following viewpoint, Jamie Mayerfeld, an associate professor of political science at the University of Washington, resists the claim that torture can be justified under certain circumstances. Criticizing the "ticking bomb" scenario, one that seeks to justify the torture of a prisoner who has information of an imminent terrorist attack, Mayerfeld believes that such events have never occurred and tend to obscure moral choice. He maintains that captors can never be certain that a prisoner has such information or that torture will yield the desired results. Lacking certainty, torturers may end up abusing an innocent person. Mayerfeld insists that the prevalent "ticking bomb" myth is something drawn from novels, movies, and television and therefore lacks real-world substantiation that could guide a moral course of action.

As you read, consider the following questions:

1. Mayerfeld attests that torture often yields false information. What are the problems he associates with acquiring false information through torture?

Jamie Mayerfeld, "In Defense of the Absolute Prohibition of Torture," *Public Affairs Quarterly*, vol. 22, no. 2, April 2008. Copyright © 2008 North American Philosophical Publications. All rights reserved. Reproduced by permission.

2. What does Mayerfeld believe a suspect in a "ticking bomb" scenario would need to ensure that the suspect was guilty beyond a reasonable doubt?

3. According to the author, "the line between self-defense and sadism becomes ever harder to see" under what speculative instances of torture?

Torture is the extreme of cruelty. One person subjects another, held captive and helpless, to terrible pain. Cruelty is combined with cowardice, because the captive not only cannot escape, but cannot fight back or retaliate. Defenselessness magnifies the captive's terror. Reduced to absolute passivity, he or she experiences, in [philosophy professor] David Sussman's apt phrase, a "living death." We do not need a lengthy discourse on the immorality of torture. If torture is not wrong, nothing is wrong. No one should be subjected to the pain and terror that torture entails.

No one defends torture as a general practice. No society gives private citizens or even public officials carte blanche to torture. (Even slave societies such as antebellum America placed legal limits on the torture of slaves, though the limits were routinely ignored.) But throughout history, states have claimed (behind closed doors, when not in public) that torture is warranted in limited circumstances. States that use torture claim that they have good reason to breach the otherwise general prohibition of torture.

To block such arguments, contemporary international law prohibits torture in all circumstances. The prohibition may never be lifted or disregarded, not even during an emergency that "threatens the life of the nation." So heinous is the crime of torture that in many countries its prosecution falls under the rubric of universal jurisdiction. This authorizes prosecution of torture committed anywhere in the world, regardless of the citizenship of the perpetrator or victim. The 145 member states of the torture convention [a United Nations agreement adopted in 1984] are obligated to prosecute any perpetrator found on their territory, or else extradite the perpetrator for prosecution in another country. The Geneva Conventions obligate all member states (now literally every country in the world) to prosecute acts of torture and inhuman treatment committed in the context of war, regardless of the citizenship of the perpetrator or victim and location of the crime.

Contemporary international law frames the absolute universal ban on torture in terms of human rights. Everyone has an absolute human right not to be tortured. "No one shall be subjected to torture or to cruel, inhuman or degrading treatment or punishment." This canonical formulation, now reproduced in many international treaties and domestic constitutions, appears first in the 1948 Universal Declaration of Human Rights, which postulates the ban as a moral imperative prior to law and derives it from the equal dignity of all human beings. The UN [Convention] Against Torture, adopted by unanimous vote of the General Assembly in 1975, states that "any act of torture or other cruel, inhuman or degrading treatment or punishment is an offense to human dignity."

Challenging the Ban on Torture

The absolute ban on torture has not gone unchallenged. Today the most common objection is that torture is sometimes warranted as a means of combating terrorism. Against the view that torture should not be used even as a means of preventing terrorism, appeal is invariably made to the ticking bomb scenario. "Imagine that a bomb has been planted that, if allowed to explode, will kill some number of innocent civilians. [Sometimes, to increase the argument's force, the number is fixed very high.] The man who planted the bomb has fallen into our custody, and refuses to tell us its location. If torturing the man is the only way for us to locate and defuse the bomb, thereby saving innocent people's lives, then aren't we morally permitted—even required—to torture him? This shows that torture is sometimes justified as a means of preventing terrorism."

The ticking bomb argument has exerted enormous influence. Popularized in books, movies, TV dramas, newspaper editorials, TV commentaries, public lectures, journal articles, college courses, and presidential debates, it has persuaded a large portion of the voting public and policy-making elite that torture is warranted on some (larger or smaller) number of occasions. It became an argument for justifying the massive use of torture by the French army during the Algerian War of Independence. It has been the primary argument for the widespread use of torture by Israeli security forces in the occupied territories. It is the main justification for the use of torture by the US government in the "war on terror."

The Fallacy of the Ticking Bomb Scenario

The fallacy of the ticking bomb argument has been repeatedly and forcefully demonstrated. Especially in the last few years, several powerful refutations have appeared in print. Anyone who is persuaded or even perplexed by the ticking bomb argument should read these works.

Several of these works make the point that the ticking bomb argument deceives us about the choices we face in the real world. The argument deceives us in two ways: by suggesting that torture could be limited to ticking bomb situations, and by suggesting that the ticking bomb situation is itself a realistic possibility. The work that most powerfully exposes the empirical deceitfulness of the ticking bomb argument is [political science professor] Darius Rejali's recently published book *Torture and Democracy*. On the basis of staggeringly thorough research, Rejali lays waste to the empirical assumptions that are implied and recirculated by the argument. Ticking bomb stories cannot be heard in the same way after one has absorbed Rejali's findings. . . .

Arguments Based in Fiction

The main goal of [this viewpoint] is to show that ticking bomb scenarios are unreal. They are unreal because they do not, in fact, occur, and because their features make it almost impossible for them to occur. The ticking bomb scenario, as we are invited to imagine it, almost certainly has never occurred and almost certainly never will occur. This point is not original, but however frequently and however well it is made, it has not sunk in. So it must be made again and again. I elaborate on the unreality of the hypothetical below. But let me here make the salient observation, which I shall repeat below, that in the long history of counterterrorist campaigns there has not been one verified report of a genuine ticking bomb torture scenario. There has not been a verified incident that even comes close to the ticking bomb torture scenario.

Among the many unrealistic elements of the ticking bomb hypothetical, I give particular attention to the exaggerated degree of certainty attributed to our belief in the prisoner's guilt. In the scenario, we are fully certain that the individual in our custody has launched an attack on civilians and is now withholding the information needed to save the civilians' lives. Such certainty is unrealistic. Any realistic approximation of the ticking bomb scenario creates too high a risk that an innocent person will be tortured.

The made-to-order features of the ticking bomb scenario blind us to torture's reality. In the real world, torture [Rejali states] "yields poor information, sweeps up many innocents, degrades organizational capabilities, and destroys interrogators." Consider the problem of false information, which not only causes delays, swallows man-hours, and leads down blind alleys, but can also encourage disastrous choices. . . .

These dangers, purged from the ticking bomb hypothetical, are inseparable from actual torture. Yet public attention is consumed by the hypothetical. Obsession with the better-than-best case scenario warps our thinking about torture. We overlook torture's dangers and exaggerate its effectiveness. By now, the ticking bomb narrative has acquired its own momentum, but fear and anger do much to keep it aloft. (When fear and anger take a racialized cast, our thinking is further distorted.)

I argue below that we should set aside the ticking bomb scenario because of its unrealistic character, that realistic approximations of the scenario pose an unacceptable risk to the innocent, that other extensions of the ticking bomb argument to more realistic scenarios not sharing its morally relevant features must be rejected, and that reasons for an absolute legal ban on torture also support an absolute moral ban on torture. . . .

Torture Becomes an Institution

[Ethics professor] Henry Shue observes that ticking bomb arguments mislead us because of idealization and abstraction:

> Idealization is the addition of positive features to an example in order to make the example better than reality, which lacks those features. Abstraction is the deletion of negative features of reality from an example in order to make the example still better than reality. Idealization adds sparkle, abstraction removes dirt. Together they make the hypothetical superior to reality and thereby a disastrously misleading analogy from which to derive conclusions about reality.

Take abstraction first. Ticking bomb arguments falsely suggest that torture could be limited to ticking bomb situations. However, torturers must be trained for their task, and can operate only with bureaucratic backing. One cannot empower the conscientious torturer without creating a cadre of bureaucratically authorized trained torturers who, from bureaucratic momentum and political and peer pressure and the desire to use their skills, will extend the practice to other situations. As Shue writes, "torture is an institution." Furthermore, as [philosophy professor Jeff] McMahan reminds us, torture in ticking bomb situations will be interpreted as a precedent for torture in non–ticking bomb situations. The ticking bomb argument imagines that torture of the terrorist will have no further effects beyond saving the civilians from the ticking bomb, but in the real world it will cause the subsequent torture of innocent people.

So torture cannot be limited to ticking bomb situations. But, and this is where idealization comes in, the ticking bomb scenario is itself a fantasy. I argue below that it is not only unrealistic, but that it almost certainly never will occur as it is standardly imagined. The hypothetical is unrealistic because it imagines that we know with certainty that our captive has planted the bomb, that although we do not know the bomb's location he does, that torture will lead him to yield the information, and that the information once gained will enable us to defuse the bomb. It is virtually impossible that we could know any of these things, much less all of them, with certainty. . . .

The Absence of Certainty

The ticking bomb scenario posits certainty that cannot be had in the real world. Some people may respond that certainty regarding all features of the hypothetical is not necessary to establish the permissibility of torture. We would, for example, be permitted to torture even if we thought it likely but not certain that torture would elicit the lifesaving information from the terrorist. But certainty on at least one point is morally required. Torture would be a grave wrong if we lacked full certainty that our captive had indeed participated in the delayed attack against the civilians and was now withholding the information needed to save the civilians' lives. (Torture might be wrong even if we possessed such certainty, but I set that question aside for now.) In the absence of full certainty, we run the risk of torturing an innocent person, and that is a morally unacceptable risk. . . .

So far are we from attaining full certainty in any realistic approximation of the ticking bomb situation, however, that we do not even rise to the level of proof beyond a reasonable doubt. To reach that standard, we would need to provide the suspected ticking bomb terrorist with a fair trial before a genuinely impartial judge and to give him full opportunities to establish his innocence or even just create reasonable doubt in the judge's mind. But the hypothetical scenario rules out any possibility of a fair trial.

And yet the ticking bomb hypothetical assumes full certainty regarding the captive's guilt. It is no accident that the hypothetical gains its primary inspiration from fiction—novels, movies, and TV shows. The conventions of fiction allow us, the readers or viewers, to know things that can never be known in real life. Facts are stipulated by the author, revealed in as many scenes as the author wishes to have us observe, undistorted by fading memory or perceptual limitations. We may even be told the characters' thoughts. The ticking bomb hypothetical confuses reality with fiction: It blurs the line between what can and cannot be known. Popular works of fiction have stoked the confusion. . . .

It is further worth remarking that discussions of the ticking bomb case tend to assume that torture can be carried out in a precise, scientific, and restrained manner; that it tends to elicit prompt actionable intelligence; that interrogators and their superiors can distinguish true tortured statements from false ones; that torture will not corrupt bureaucracies; and that it will not alienate populations from which the torture victims are drawn. These assumptions are illusory. They are additional myths that are reinforced by the ticking bomb argument. . . .

Torture on Assumption That a Prisoner Has Information

Ticking bomb scenarios do not occur in real life. But some writers say that the intuitions elicited by them show us that torture is morally permitted (or even required) in other more realistic cases. The idea seems to be that if we have captured a known terrorist, torture need not be confined to actual ticking bomb situations. We may torture him even if we are not fully certain but only think that there *may* be a ticking bomb plot, or that he *may* have the knowledge necessary to abort it. Even if there is no ticking bomb, we may torture him for information about his organization's infrastructure—information that will help us achieve our long-term goal of destroying the organization. In [conservative columnist Charles] Krauthammer's words, torture is sometimes warranted for slow-fuse as well as ticking bombs.

These are scary proposals. We claim the moral right to torture even if, *as we acknowledge*, there may well be no ticking bomb plot to abort, or our captive may well have no relevant information to give, or the information sought may well be unnecessary to prevent an actual attack. The captive's past crime becomes our continuing license to torture him for speculative gain. This carries our dehumanization of him to a new level—far beyond that contemplated in the fanciful ticking bomb case. The line between self-defense and sadism becomes ever harder to see. Notice that such reasoning places no temporal limit on a person's torture. We may, in principle, torture someone for months or years—possibly the rest of his or her life. Guantánamo Bay [the US detention facility in Cuba that holds prisoners of the wars in Afghanistan and Iraq] is the hellish incarnation of the slow-fuse bomb justification of torture.

Meanwhile, all the earlier noted problems remain, though now in magnified form. We lack full certainty that our captive is in fact a terrorist. The institutional dynamics of torture will lead us to torture even more widely than our now greatly broadened rubric, so that many entirely innocent people will be tortured. Our practice will encourage others to torture with even less restraint. The view that terrorism makes its practitioners broadly liable to torture may be extended, in logic not always easy to refute, to crimes (or alleged crimes) other than terrorism. The broader use of torture will impede the struggle against terrorism, even stimulate terrorism. It will brutalize the torturers, causing abuse to spread in families, police cells, and military barracks. . . .

Believing in the Unreal

Individuals, like institutions, are too prone to error. Fear, anger, racism, and bombardment by government and media messages distort our perceptions, predisposing us to see ticking bombs where they do not exist. The constant recirculation of the ticking bomb story increases our suggestibility. Above all, there is the extreme unlikelihood of the ticking bomb situation itself. Add to that our incurable tendency to exaggerate the certainty of our beliefs. The upshot is that if you think you are faced with a ticking bomb scenario—there is a ticking bomb, the person in your custody has planted it, etc.,—there is a very high probability that you are wrong. This alone is a strong argument that you should never torture.

"*Soulless leadership anguishes over the marketplace image that creates publicity and influence, not the genuine suffering and injustice behind it.*"

Torture Reveals America's Loss of Principles in the Iraq War

Edward Tick

In the following viewpoint, Edward Tick contends that the instances of torture that occurred during the US invasion and occupation of Iraq are not isolated injustices. Instead, Tick sees them as part of a historical legacy of abuse perpetrated by soldiers operating under the dehumanizing atmosphere of war. More importantly, though, Tick believes that the US government's condemnation of the soldiers' acts during the Iraq war was disingenuous. He maintains that in calling the abuse "un-American," the presidential administration of George W. Bush was more interested in saving the face of the nation than addressing the suffering of the victims and the immorality of the war. Tick argues that the war in Iraq has little moral justification, and therefore, America's troops are left ethically adrift on a mission that seems to have no honorable purpose. Edward Tick is the founding director of Soldier's Heart, an organization that provides support to veterans and their families. He is the author of several books on spiritual healing, including War and the Soul: Healing Our Nation's Veterans from Post-Traumatic Stress Disorder.

As you read, consider the following questions:

1. In Tick's view, who is ultimately responsible in wartime to differentiate between military orders that must be obeyed and those that are criminal and inhumane?

2. Who first coined the phrase "atrocity-producing situation," as Tick states?

3. According to Tick, what is it that President George W. Bush and his administration never seemed to grasp about the torture cases and all else that went wrong in the war in Iraq?

One thing that has gone *right* in the war in Iraq has been various disclosures of torture and sadism by American troops against Iraqi prisoners. We must never rationalize or condone such acts. We must not, as Pres. [George W.] Bush did when the Abu Ghraib prison scandal was first revealed[1], claim that "they do not represent the America that I know." We must not, as Sec. [of Defense Donald] Rumsfeld did, label them as "fundamentally un-American" and something our troops would not do. Such rhetorical ploys only shift blame from higher officials and the cause itself to the ordinary American servicemen and women on the front lines who did the deeds. And we must not, as Bush and [Vice President Dick] Cheney have been doing for months, justify torture as a means for extracting valuable information. Experience from

---

1. In 2004 members of a US military police unit were accused and later convicted of abusing Iraqi prisoners held in the Abu Ghraib detention facility on the outskirts of Baghdad.

© 2009 by Andy Singer and PoliticalCartoons.com.

history and from many wars demonstrates that torture strengthens, not weakens, both individual and collective resistance. And it has no rational or humane justification.

Bringing Atrocities to Light

It is right that atrocities are exposed in war. Only months passed from the time of the Abu Ghraib prison abuse until it was reported to the world. During the Vietnam War, the My Lai Massacre [committed by US soldiers against civilians] did not rock the country until we were in that war, officially, for seven years. A full year had passed before the atrocity was exposed. The No Gun Ri Massacre [of Korean refugees by US troops] that occurred during the Korean War was only revealed by groundbreaking journalism at the beginning of this millennium, half a century after it occurred. Edward Bloch, an 80-year-old veteran and Marine platoon leader in the Pacific during World War II, declares that he will not die in peace until he is able, against official resistance, to document and get into the history books the massacre of a village he participated in in cooperation with defeated Japanese troops on mainland China after his war's end. It is necessary for the ultimate health and safety of the troops on the front lines and the civilization at home that whenever there is war, atrocities are exposed as early and often as possible.

This is not to condemn soldiers who commit them. Military law states that it is ultimately each soldier's duty to differentiate those orders that might be criminal and unduly inhumane from normal military orders that must be obeyed. GIs [service members] are responsible for their actions and must be accountable. But we must not demonize them, as Mr. Bush did, as aberrations. Most of the offenders at Abu Ghraib were ordinary Americans, not sadists or psychopaths. Rather, the occurrence of atrocities during wartime force us to try to confront what any of us, our neighbors or our children, can become and do, and that certain conditions will bring out the worst of our society and human nature.

Examining What Makes Soldiers Commit Torture and Abuse

Psychological research shows that only about 2% of the American population are psychopaths or have psychopathic tendencies. These tendencies attract some people to the military where they may do well if they receive enough structure and authoritative guidance. But their destructive tendencies can be unleashed without restraint or remorse in combat and other social conditions produced in a war environment. It is unlikely that torture is only perpetrated by a gathering of that 2%. If so, we would have to ask how and why they gathered, and take measures to ensure that military planners do not group soldiers with psychopathic tendencies in the same unit. More realistically, we must assume that, in this Iraq war as in wars of the past, most service people who have stripped, beaten, molested, raped, humiliated, tied and killed prisoners were ordinary people who became extraordinarily distorted. What drives people to such acts?

Examining these questions about Vietnam veterans during that war, psychiatrist Robert Jay Lifton, author of *Home from the War*, first coined the phrase "atrocity-producing situation." When fear, threat, violence suffered and given, loss, proximity of death, moral confusion, alienation, disbelief, immersion in horror, power and control over others, sheer exhaustion of body, mind, and spirit all coincide long enough, and when the enemy has been steadily and sufficiently dehumanized . . . , then we are in an atrocity-producing situation. Only extraordinary people resist and it can take extraordinary means. One GI shot himself in the foot so that he wouldn't participate in the killings at My Lai. In both the Vietnam and Iraq wars, GIs who reported these tortures were concerned about retaliations against them but decided on higher moral actions than "following orders" and keeping silent. But many ordinarily decent people will succumb to the level of the environmental conditions surrounding them. They may act out the ugliest, most sadistic dimensions of what depth psychologists call the human shadow. Most of us, when conditions force it, can become uncivilized and can humiliate, shame, abuse and destroy. Some of us, when conditions allow it, may take these emotions of war and the beast within to intolerable extremes.

Facing the Horror as a Nation

When nations behave as colonial powers, [journalist] Philip Kennicott wrote in the *Washington Post* when the Abu Ghraib prison scandal was first exposed in 2004, demeaning occupied people, insulting their traditions, humiliating them, it is "not surprising . . . unexceptional"; atrocity is the inevitable extension of colonialism. And when soldiers do not believe in what they are asked to do, when they are not sure that killing is justified or that its cause is morally incontrovertible, when they cannot bolster themselves with supreme principles against their destruction of farms and villages, cities and holy sites, and against maiming and killing helpless civilians along with enemy combatants, then we will inevitably see atrocity. It was perpetrated by the Dutch in Indonesia, the Belgians in the [Democratic Republic of the] Congo, by the Turks against the Armenians, the Japanese and Germans before and during World War II. It was perpetrated by the French in Indochina and Algeria, by Russians in Afghanistan, by Israelis and Palestinians against each other, by Americans against Native Americans, and in Korea, Vietnam, and now in Iraq. "What you do, you become," wrote Vietnam veteran Gustav Hasford in *The Short-Timers*, his novel of jungle combat. When the character Kurtz, in both Joseph Conrad's novel *Heart of Darkness* and [Francis Ford] Coppola's Vietnam War movie *Apocalypse Now*, muttered "The horror, the horror," he was not looking at the war around him but within. Wars inevitably produce atrocity because soldiers steeped in horror for a long enough period of time will finally become that horror.

American leaders, in their early responses to the disclosure of torture, used denial and the marginalizing and blaming of individuals. As Kennicott wrote regarding Abu Ghraib, "The problem isn't the abuse of the prisoners . . . we're not really like that. The problem is our reputation. Our soldiers' reputations. Our national self-image. These photos, we insist, are not us." In the debate over the continued use of torture and the leadership's resistance to Sen. [John] McCain's proposed law banning torture, Bush administration officials have been using rationalization and justification. Torture, claim Cheney and Rumsfeld, furthers our cause by providing valuable information. These leaders, by and large, express concern not with the unjust sufferings of our victimized prisoners, but with furthering their own agenda and shaping the image of our nation and our soldiers around the world. Sen. McCain has been concerned about America's loss of moral prestige in the eyes of the world. On Bush's final tentative agreement to support his proposed ban on torture, he said, "We've sent a message to the world that the United States is not like the terrorists.... What we are is a nation that upholds values and standards...." Pres. Bush and his associates never seem to grasp that all that has gone wrong in this war and in the world's opinion of our nation are direct consequences of this war. Soulless leadership anguishes over the marketplace image that creates publicity and influence, not the genuine suffering and injustice behind it.

It is not true that atrocities and torture are "un-American" or inconsistent with American values. Rather, such acts show shadow aspects of this war and our soldiers' beliefs about its morality and justification. They demonstrate the moral confusion and deterioration of our troops in the combat zone and about their mission and purpose. They show the worst side of us as Americans and human beings under conditions that encourage the worst to triumph over the best in the human spirit. That is the kind of war we've created. That is what can happen to our children when we send them off to this kind of war. And what happens to our children, and how they will suffer for the rest of their lives, may be the best index we have for the true spirit of this war.

"Congress should resist initiatives that would repeal or erode key provisions of the Patriot Act and should fully institutionalize these tools into the broader counterterrorism framework."

America Should Use Its Surveillance Tools to Preserve National Security

Jena Baker McNeill

The USA PATRIOT Act, commonly referred to as the Patriot Act, is a piece of US legislation designed to aid in the surveillance of suspected terrorists by permitting the government to conduct wiretaps and access telecommunications records, employment files, and other background information. In the following viewpoint, Jena Baker McNeill argues that the Patriot Act has helped keep the nation safe since its initial passage in 2001. In 2009, when some of the provisions of the act were due to expire, McNeill urged Congress, in this viewpoint, to reauthorize key elements in hopes that the act would continue to serve national security. These provisions were extended and signed into

Jena Baker McNeill, "Patriot Act: A Chance to Commit to National Security," Heritage Foundation WebMemo #2648, October 9, 2009. Copyright © 2009 by Heritage Foundation.

law by President Barack Obama. Jena Baker McNeill is a senior policy analyst on homeland security at the Heritage Foundation, a conservative public policy research institute.

As you read, consider the following questions:

1. What is the function of the roving surveillance provision of the Patriot Act, according to McNeill?

2. How is Section 215 of the Patriot Act different from a grand jury subpoena, as McNeill emphasizes?

3. Quoting then attorney general John Ashcroft, McNeill states that the Patriot Act has been instrumental in the arrest of how many terrorism suspects since its passage?

On September 22–23 [2009], the House and Senate Judiciary Committees held hearings to examine reauthorization of key provisions of the Patriot Act [also known as the USA PATRIOT Act], which helps law enforcement fight terrorism through more flexible surveillance and investigation methods and easier information sharing. Key provisions of the act will expire on December 31 [2009] if Congress does not reauthorize them.

The three foiled terrorist plots announced this past week [in early October 2009] are evidence that America's counterterrorism tools are working. And the Patriot Act is a key element in this framework. Not only does it help fight terrorism by aiding authorities in their effort to stop the flow of information and resources between terrorist groups, but it does so in a way that is consistent with the U.S. Constitution. This tool should be supported and maintained by Congress.

Important Provisions of the Patriot Act

The Patriot Act, enacted shortly after the attacks on 9/11 [referring to the September 11, 2001, terrorist attacks on the United States], was intended to help law enforcement share information as well as to provide more extensive methods by which to track down terrorists at the earliest stages of terrorist plot formation. The act makes it easier for authorities to conduct surveillance on terrorists, with key provisions that account for modern technologies (such as cell phones). While there are multiple provisions that make up the Patriot Act, there are three provisions set to expire this year:

1. *Section 206: Roving Surveillance Authority.* This provision allows law enforcement, after approval from the court created by the Foreign Intelligence Surveillance Act (FISA), to conduct continuous surveillance of national security suspects across modes of communications. It is meant to stop terrorists who often switch telecommunications devices (like cell phones) to evade authorities.

While roving surveillance has been available to authorities in criminal investigations prior to 2001, Section 206 would allow authorities to perform such an act in national security investigations. This gives law enforcement flexibility, but it does so with built-in procedural safeguards, such as a requirement that the requesting authority demonstrate probable cause for the surveillance.

It further requires continuous monitoring by the FISA court and extensive oversight by Congress. This section, used approximately 140 times since 2001, is a gigantic step forward in terms of helping law enforcement fight terrorism in a modern, technological world.

2. *Section 215: Business Record Orders under FISA.* This provision allows law enforcement, with approval from the FISA court, to require disclosure of documents and other records from businesses and other institutions (third parties) without a suspect's knowledge.

It is essentially a way for prosecutors to obtain evidence in national security investigations in a fashion similar to that of a grand jury subpoena. The difference is that Section 215 actually requires more procedural safeguards than a grand jury subpoena, including a requirement that the requesting authority show relevance and obtain court approval (the grand jury standard being a simple showing of relevance).

It further protects civil liberties by requiring additional approval for document requests that might have the slightest relation to freedom of speech and expression, such as library records. It has been used approximately 250 times since 9/11.

3. *Section 6001 of the Intelligence Reform and Terrorism Prevention Act: The Lone Wolf Provision.* This provision allows law enforcement to track non-U.S. citizens acting alone to commit acts of terrorism that are not connected to an organized terrorist group or other foreign power. While the FBI [Federal Bureau of Investigation] has confirmed that this section has never actually been used, it needs to be available if the situation arises where a lone individual may seek to do harm to the United States.

The Patriot Act Is Successful at Foiling Terrorist Plots

The U.S. has not experienced a terrorist attack on its own soil since 9/11, despite repeated attempts. In fact, an examination of publicly available information demonstrates that at least 26 terrorist plots have been foiled since 9/11.

The 2002 Lackawanna Six plot, where individuals involved in the drug trade went overseas to obtain terrorist training, was foiled partly because law enforcement was able to pursue the investigation as a single case, a luxury afforded to them only because of changes made under the Patriot Act. Under a pre–Patriot Act standard, law enforcement would have been required to pursue the drug investigation separately from the terrorism plot, unable to share information and evidence acquired.

Attorney General John Ashcroft has credited the Patriot Act as a major factor in the arrest of 310 terrorism suspects.

And just this week, the success of the Patriot Act was recognized by President Barack Obama when he expressed his support for its reauthorization.

While the FBI has not indicated whether this week's foiled plots were the result of the Patriot Act's provisions, a spokesman stated that he could not discuss the tools used to investigate the case because these authorities were before the FISA court.

Despite repeated attempts to demonstrate abuse, little evidence has ever been proffered to demonstrate any Patriot Act misuse. In fact, at times the Patriot Act offers significantly more protections than available under common criminal investigations. And more often than not, it simply modernizes already available tools that prosecutors have used routinely in criminal investigations well before 2001. These provisions are subject to routine oversight by both the FISA court and Congress. The act has been narrowed and refined continuously, contributing to the fact that no single provision of the Patriot Act has ever been found unconstitutional.

Congress should resist initiatives that would repeal or erode key provisions of the Patriot Act and should fully institutionalize these tools into the broader counterterrorism framework. As former White House homeland security adviser Ken Weinstein phrased it, "There is no reason to return to the days when it was easier for prosecutors to secure records in a simple assault prosecution than for national security investigators to obtain records that may help prevent the next 9/11."

> *"We have to speak up now, before our surveillance society is irrevocably entrenched and we find that we have permanently sacrificed our essential values."*

National Security Tools Should Not Infringe on Civil Liberties

American Civil Liberties Union

The American Civil Liberties Union (ACLU) is a nonpartisan institution that provides educational and legal services to redress perceived abuses of civil rights. In the following viewpoint, the ACLU contends that the US government's broad surveillance powers granted under the USA PATRIOT Act, commonly known as the Patriot Act, are a threat to privacy and individual liberty. According to the organization, the Patriot Act allows government security agencies to secretly investigate personal records and collect any information on Americans who, in the opinion of these agencies, are engaged in suspicious activities that may be a risk to national security. The ACLU believes the oversight and restraints on this profiling are too vague and simply permit the

government to amass private data as it sees fit. Furthermore, the
ACLU claims that the surveillance powers have not demonstra-
tively kept Americans any safer from terrorists or other wrongdo-
ers since the passage of the law.

As you read, consider the following questions:

1. How did the Patriot Act alter the scope of surveillance
   powers granted by preexisting national security letters,
   in the ACLU's view?

2. What does government "data mining" seek to do, according to the ACLU?

3. Of the 150,000 NSL requests made by the FBI between
   2003 and 2005, how many of these figured into a conviction of a suspect in a terrorism case?

Privacy rights in America are based on the fundamental
principle that our government must have *actual suspicion*
that someone is breaking the law or actively preparing to do
so before monitoring Americans in our daily activities. It is
not enough for government to decide to spy on us *just in case*
we are engaged in wrongdoing. And just as importantly, usually a judge has to agree with the justification and authorize
the surveillance *before* it begins. Put simply, our Constitution
protects us from unwarranted government intrusion into our
private lives.

But under pressure from the executive branch to fight terrorism, Congress has weakened Americans' privacy protections—and profoundly altered our relationship to our government. In the atmosphere of widespread fear that followed 9/11
[referring to the September 11, 2001, terrorist attacks on the
United States], the [George W.] Bush administration asked
Congress to loosen critical constraints on surveillance under
which the intelligence community and law enforcement agencies had long operated—without ever demonstrating that
those constraints contributed to the attacks. After barely any

debate, Congress granted the Bush administration the authority it sought in the form of the USA PATRIOT Act. Using Patriot Act authority, the Bush administration started—and the [Barack] Obama administration has continued—to conduct wholesale "preventive" surveillance of innocent Americans without judicial review.

Not Enough Restraints on Patriot Act Powers

For example, the Patriot Act expanded the FBI's [Federal Bureau of Investigation's] authority to use "national security letters" (NSLs) to secretly demand telecommunications, credit, and financial information from private companies about not just suspected terrorists, but anyone the FBI deemed "relevant" to an FBI investigation. Before 9/11, the FBI already had the authority to use NSLs to obtain information about suspected spies or international terrorists, but the Patriot Act's significant change was to remove the requirement that the FBI actually suspect that a person about whom it collected information was engaged in wrongdoing. Without that key constraint, the FBI engaged in flagrant violations of law. And Congress has been complicit in those violations because it has exercised its oversight authority enough to be on notice that violations are occurring, but not enough to curb them.

Thus, in 2005, when Congress was debating whether to extend expiring provisions of the Patriot Act, it called Attorney General Alberto Gonzales and FBI Director Robert Mueller to testify about the FBI's use of its authorities; both stated that there were no "substantiated" allegations of abuse. Because the FBI exercised its Patriot Act powers in complete secrecy, often enforced through unconstitutional gag orders, Congress had no way to verify these claims, so it reauthorized the Patriot Act, but ordered an audit of the FBI's use of its powers. The Department of Justice inspector general released five damning audit reports, revealing thousands of violations of law and policy. Despite the evidence of the FBI's widespread and years-long misuse of its Patriot Act authority, Congress has failed to retract any of the sweeping powers it granted and has repeatedly reauthorized all expiring Patriot Act provisions without narrowing them in any way.

The Obama administration, like the Bush administration before it, has used excessive secrecy to hide possibly unconstitutional surveillance. Two members of Congress have been ringing alarm bells about the government's use of Patriot Act authorities, urging additional congressional oversight—to no avail. Hobbled by executive claims of secrecy, Senators Ron Wyden and Mark Udall have nevertheless warned their colleagues that the government is operating under a "reinterpretation" of the Patriot Act that is so broad that the public will be stunned and angered by its scope, and that the executive branch is engaging in dragnet surveillance in which "innocent Americans are getting swept up." History threatens to repeat itself. But the American public deserves more than another secret showdown; and we should not have to rely on government whistleblowers to come forward at the risk of criminal prosecution, to act as a check and balance on an unaccountable executive.

Collecting a Host of Personal Data on Americans

Nothing exemplifies the risks our national surveillance society poses to our privacy rights better than government "data mining." Data mining is based on the dubious and unproven premise that "terrorist patterns" can be ferreted out from the enormous mass of American lives, which, of course, are quirky, eccentric, and may be riddled with what look like suspicious coincidences but are actually innocent activities.

In 2002, for example, the American public found out that the Pentagon was working on a project to gather information from thousands of government and commercial databases worldwide, covering every facet of our lives, with the goal of aggregating our personal information into one giant database that military and law enforcement officials could search for "suspect activity" related to terrorism. That program was called, aptly enough, "Total Information Awareness" (TIA), and it remains the paradigm for how new technology may be used to bring us closer to the nightmare of routine mass government surveillance of our daily activities. After TIA became public, Americans from across the political spectrum raised their voices in opposition, and Congress shut the program down. But Congress then ignored the public's demand for privacy protections and allowed key data-mining elements of TIA to be perpetuated under the secret umbrella of the NSA [National Security Agency], where we cannot monitor their use.

Government data mining is now being replicated in a variety of other programs at the federal, state, and local levels, to spy on Americans in virtually complete secrecy. So-called "suspicious activity reporting" programs, for example, maintain that innocuous and commonplace behavior like photography and note taking about public buildings could be preparation to conduct terrorist attacks, and that the government should collect and retain information about Americans who engage in these activities. The range and number of these programs is breathtaking and their names Orwellian [referring to George Orwell's novel 1984, in which a free and open society is challenged]. Programs such as eGuardian, "Eagle Eyes," "Patriot Reports," and "See Something, Say Something" are now run by agencies including the Director of National Intelligence, the FBI, the Department of Defense, and the Department of Homeland Security. State and local law enforcement agencies often have their own, similar programs. And once the government collects data about "suspicious" activity, it can retain it for a lifetime, even when the information shows the person is not a threat.

Without effective oversight, security agencies are now also engaged in a "land grab," rushing into the legal vacuum to expand their monitoring powers far beyond anything seen in our history. Each of the over 300 million cell phones in the United States, for example, reveals its location to the mobile network carrier with ever-increasing accuracy, whenever it is turned on, and the Justice Department is aggressively using cell phones to monitor people's location, claiming that it does not need a warrant. With thousands of government requests coming to private telecommunications carriers every month, Sprint Nextel even set up a dedicated website so that law-enforcement agents can access our location records from their desks.

Surveillance Programs Have Done Little for Americans' Safety

Yet for all the privacy we have relinquished in the name of preventing terrorism, and for all the national treasure spent on surveillance, we are no safer. Our political leaders urge the necessity of surveillance and data-mining programs by posing a false choice between our privacy and our safety. Each time Congress is due to reexamine expiring Patriot Act provisions, for example, government officials warn in the direst tones that without secret surveillance and data collection, our nation's security will be jeopardized. We cannot fully evaluate these warnings because of secrecy constraints, but internal investigations make clear that the warnings are infused with baseless fearmongering. For example, a combined review of the NSA's secret wiretapping by inspectors general at key security agencies was unable to turn up any evidence that the program made us safer, despite its unprecedented scope. The same is true for national security letters. From 2003 to 2005, the FBI made close to 150,000 NSL requests. But the FBI inspector general documented only one conviction in a terrorism case

The Perils of Infringing on Civil Liberties

We ... know that without sufficient limits and oversight, well-meaning efforts to keep the homeland safe—efforts which rely heavily on the collection and analysis of significant amounts of information about Americans—can adversely impact civil liberties. Indeed, history teaches that insufficiently checked domestic investigative powers frequently have been abused and that the burdens of this abuse most often fall upon disfavored communities and those with unpopular political views. Investigations triggered by race, ethnicity, religious belief, or political ideology may seem calibrated to address the threat we face, but instead they routinely target innocent people and groups. Beyond the harm done to individuals, such investigations invade privacy, chill religious belief, radicalize communities and, ultimately, build resistance to cooperation with law enforcement.

Emily Berman, "Domestic Intelligence: New Powers, New Risk," Brennan Center for Justice at New York University School of Law, January 18, 2011.

using data from NSLs during the three-year period, and found no instance in which an NSL request helped to prevent an actual terrorist plot.

There is thus little or no evidence of additional plots foiled, arrests made, or lives saved as a result of data mining and mass surveillance programs. The reality is that as governmental surveillance has become easier and less constrained, security agencies are flooded with junk data, generating thousands of false leads that distract from real threats. In the name of finding the terrorist needle in a haystack, our government has built the biggest haystack in history—and it is growing all the time.

Speak Up for the Right to Speak Up

Too often, post-9/11 government surveillance has targeted people for expressing political opinions or protesting government policies. The ACLU has documented examples of political spying, monitoring, and harassment of Americans based on their First Amendment–protected activities by federal, state, and local officials in at least 33 states and the District of Columbia. The government has spied on racial and religious minority groups and community organizations, college groups, military reservists calling home to their families, journalists, aid workers, political activists, and many others.

It is not too late to strengthen our laws, to take back our data, and to ensure that government surveillance is conducted under effective and reasonable constraints, subject to meaningful oversight. But we have to speak up now, before our surveillance society is irrevocably entrenched and we find that we have permanently sacrificed our essential values. Otherwise, we risk changing our national character and surrendering one of the key freedoms we strive to protect—our right to privacy and our ability to speak, dissent, exchange ideas, and engage in political activity without the chilling fear of unwarranted government intrusion.

Periodical Bibliography

The following articles have been selected to supplement the diverse views presented in this chapter.

Moustafa Bayoumi — "Between Acceptance and Rejection: Muslim Americans and the Legacies of September 11," *OAH Magazine of History*, July 2011.

Fred Branfman — "On Torture and Being 'Good Americans,'" *Huffington Post*, March 2, 2006.

Darrell Cole — "Torture and Just War," *Journal of Religious Ethics*, March 2012.

David Cole — "The War on Civil Liberties," *Nation*, July 18, 2011.

Amos N. Guiora — "Human Rights and Counterterrorism: A Contradiction or Necessary Bedfellows?," *Georgia Law Review*, Spring 2012.

Michael Isikoff — "The Snitch in Your Pocket," *Newsweek*, February 18, 2010.

Regina Karp — "Nuclear Disarmament: Should America Lead?," *Political Science Quarterly*, Spring 2012.

Keith B. Payne — "Disarmament Danger," *National Review*, April 19, 2010.

Nancy Soderberg and Ryan Costello — "President Obama's Nuclear Legacy," *American Foreign Policy Interests*, June 2012.

Evan Thomas — "The Debate Over Torture," *Newsweek*, November 21, 2005.

For Further Discussion

Chapter 1

1. Richard N. Haass contends that just war theory is too restrictive, keeping governments from acting swiftly to counter threats. According to Haass, what ethics should guide governments in justifying military action? Do you agree with his concept of a justified war? Why or why not? Read Robert Higgs's viewpoint in the chapter before explaining your answer.

2. This chapter contains two viewpoints on preventive war. After rereading these viewpoints, explain whether you think preventive war can be just. If you accept preventive war as a valid policy, then define the circumstances under which you think it can be justified. Additionally, cite any dangers you think might be associated with a preventive war policy. If you disagree with preventive war as a national policy, explain why and point out what hazards exist by abandoning it.

3. Susan Brooks Thistlethwaite and Brian Katulis maintain that America's moral justification for the war in Afghanistan suffers from unclear objectives and lack of international sanction. Ryan King simply argues the war is unjust because the US government failed to exhaust all options before embarking on military action. Reread these viewpoints and do additional research online to find out what analysts and policy makers have said about the justifications for the war in Afghanistan. Then, using support from these experts, give your opinion on whether America is justified in being involved in that country and whether Washington needs to make clear its aims to the US public and the world community.

Chapter 2

1. Thomas Lawfield claims that disputes over water access have led more often to treaties than conflict. He expects that such negotiations will continue to define water management even as water scarcity becomes a more pressing issue in world affairs. What kind of evidence does Lawfield give to support his prediction?

2. Similar to the arguments about looming water wars presented in this chapter, Michael T. Klare and Daniel Yergin provide opposing views on the possibility that access to energy reserves might cause global conflict as these resources decline. Klare takes the view that nations will stake claim to energy resources and control them for their own profit and security. Yergin, on the other hand, believes that it is in the best interests of all nations to work cooperatively to secure energy stocks so that all may benefit from them. Using the arguments in these viewpoints and any others you may find, explain whether you think that, in a future world of declining energy stocks, nations will seek to hoard energy resources or cooperate and share them.

3. Alan Lurie has a religious background as an ordained rabbi. Knowing this, do you think his religious view informs his viewpoint in the chapter? Give examples of where you think his religious outlook colors his opinion of the potential for violence in fundamentalist religions.

Chapter 3

1. America declared war on terrorism immediately after al Qaeda terrorists crashed airliners into the World Trade Center and the Pentagon on September 11, 2001. Several years into that ongoing war, Juan Zarate and Justin Raimondo offer differing opinions on whether the United States and its allies are winning the war on terrorism. What kinds of evidence does each author provide to sup-

port his claim regarding the war on terror? Whose evidence do you find more conclusive? Explain why. Then, detail any other incidents or arguments you have come across that are not contained in these authors' viewpoints but have helped shaped your outlook on America's success or failure in the war on terror.

2. William McCants and William Rosenau maintain that after years on the run from the vengeance of America and its allies, al Qaeda has proven ineffectual in carrying out another significant terrorist attack on American soil. The authors believe it is time for the US government to declare victory against the defeated al Qaeda network. Seth G. Jones, on the other hand, claims that it is too early to declare victory because al Qaeda has been resilient even under intense pressure, recruiting members and forming alliances with national governments. Since the 9/11 attacks on the United States, do you think al Qaeda is still a threat or should America declare victory over a defeated organization? What evidence found in these viewpoints has influenced your opinion? Explain.

3. Karen J. Greenberg insists that America should cease the war on terrorism and end the indefinite detention of prisoners to convince the American public and the world that it respects the rule of law. Do you think her argument should guide how and when the US government declares an end to the war on terror? Are there other reasons to end the war or continue the fight that Greenberg does not focus upon but that have influenced your views on the subject? Explain your answer.

Chapter 4

1. In 2009 President Barack Obama announced his hopes that America, working with other global nuclear powers, could bring about a world free of nuclear weapons. Focusing on US-Russian agreements, Obama anticipated reduc-

ing the nuclear arsenals in both countries over time. In 2010 Russia and the United States signed the New Strategic Arms Reduction Treaty (New START) that set limits on nuclear warheads and missile launchers. Some see the treaty as another step closer to realizing Obama's goal. Others fear the reduction of nuclear capabilities will weaken US national security and jeopardize the protection of vital allies. Using the first two viewpoints in this chapter, describe whether you believe America should continue to reduce its arsenal or reconsider this policy. Explain what you think are the most important reasons for retaining or reducing nuclear arms and what would be at stake if the US government adopted your strategy.

2. After reading the three central viewpoints in this chapter, describe why the United States should or should not condone torture as a method of ensuring national security. Explain what principles guide your decision. You may use the arguments in the viewpoints to support your reasoning.

3. Jena Baker McNeill contends that the USA PATRIOT Act and other surveillance tools put in place since the terrorist attacks of September 2001 are necessary measures to keep America safe. The American Civil Liberties Union, however, argues that these laws and provisions have eroded democracy in the United States by permitting the government unimpeded access to personal information. After reading both viewpoints, could you devise a way to permit the surveillance of suspected terrorists without intruding on the liberties of innocent Americans? What safeguards do you think need to be in place to maintain effective surveillance without sacrificing civil liberties? In forming your answer, be sure to decide ultimately if the Patriot Act should continue to be enforced or if it should be repealed.

Organizations to Contact

The editors have compiled the following list of organizations concerned with the issues debated in this book. The descriptions are derived from materials provided by the organizations. All have publications or information available for interested readers. The list was compiled on the date of publication of the present volume; the information provided here may change. Be aware that many organizations take several weeks or longer to respond to inquiries, so allow as much time as possible.

Act Now to Stop War and End Racism (ANSWER)
617 Florida Avenue NW, Lower Level, Washington, DC 20001
(202) 265-1948
e-mail: info@internationalanswer.org
website: www.internationalanswer.org

Act Now to Stop War and End Racism (ANSWER) is a national coalition of organizations dedicated to ending war and racism internationally and advocating on behalf of working and poor people in the United States. Following the terrorist attacks on September 11, 2001, ANSWER began working to foster the antiwar movement within the United States. The organization has called for an end to what it views as the Israeli war on Gaza and also has called for a withdrawal of US forces from Afghanistan, which would end the war there. Articles detailing these positions, including "Palestine Holds Strong in the Face of US-Backed Israeli Terror Campaign" and "Why Rebellions Are Sweeping the Middle East, Africa and Asia," can be read on the ANSWER website.

American Enterprise Institute for Public Policy Research (AEI)
1150 Seventh Street NW, Washington, DC 20036
(202) 862-5800 • fax: (202) 862-7177
website: www.aei.org

The nonpartisan American Enterprise Institute for Public Policy Research (AEI) conducts research and educates both policy makers and the public on issues including the US government, politics, economy, and social welfare. AEI has produced extensive content relating to a variety of wars and conflicts existing in the world today with emphasis on the wars in Afghanistan and Iraq and the ongoing conflicts throughout the Middle East, as well as on tensions between Japan and China. Articles detailing the events in all these regions can be read on the AEI website and in the monthly magazine of the organization, the *American.*

Amnesty International
5 Penn Plaza, New York, NY   10001
(212) 807-8400 • fax: (212) 627-1451
e-mail: aimember@aiusa.org
website: www.amnesty.org

Amnesty International is a global organization consisting of members, activists, and supporters who work on an international scale to combat human rights abuses and protect the rights all humans are guaranteed by both the Universal Declaration of Human Rights and other human rights standards. One recurring cause of human rights abuses within the organization's literature is war. Articles relating to the human rights abuses that have resulted from war crimes or that have occurred in connection with protecting national security can be read on Amnesty International's website.

Arms Control Association (ACA)
1313 L Street NW, Suite 130, Washington, DC   20005
(202) 463-8270 • fax: (202) 463-8273
e-mail: aca@armscontrol.org
website: www.armscontrol.org

Since its founding in 1971, the Arms Control Association (ACA) has worked to provide educational materials to the public that promote effective arms control policies, with a major goal being nuclear nonproliferation and disarmament.

Other areas of focus by the ACA include biological and chemical weapons, missile defense and testing, tactical nuclear weapons, and US nuclear weapons and policy. In addition to the multiple publications on these topics, ACA Threat Assessment Briefs provide a detailed look at specific security threats and make suggestions about how the government should respond to these threats. All these materials can be accessed on ACA's website.

Cato Institute
1000 Massachusetts Avenue NW
Washington, DC 20001-5403
(202) 842-0200 • fax: (202) 842-3490
website: www.cato.org

The Cato Institute is a libertarian public policy think tank that espouses the beliefs of individual liberty, limited government, free markets, and peace. In its focus on national security and foreign policy, Cato promotes policy that protects the country but does not engage in empire building or interventionist strategies. Cato experts who write on this topic explore the range of conflict around the globe in regions including Asia and the Middle East and on topics such as terrorism and homeland security. Articles exploring these issues can be read on the Cato website.

Council on Foreign Relations (CFR)
The Harold Pratt House, 58 East Sixty-Eighth Street
New York, NY 10065
(212) 434-9400 • fax: (212) 434-9800
website: www.cfr.org

The Council on Foreign Relations (CFR) has operated for nearly a decade as a nonpartisan, independent public policy organization that strives to produce trustworthy analysis of a wide range of international issues for policy makers, business leaders, journalists, students, and citizens. CFR's work on war spans a range of issues including defense and homeland security, proliferation, and terrorism; additionally, the organization focuses specifically on international peace and security. CFR has conducted extensive research on issues relating to this topic, including the Israeli-Palestinian conflict, tension in Asia, Iranian nuclear weapons, and unrest in the Middle East. Articles on all these topics and many more can be found on the CFR's website.

Federation of American Scientists (FAS)
1725 DeSales Street NW, Suite 600, Washington, DC   20036
(202) 546-3300 • fax: (202) 675-1010
e-mail: fas@fas.org
website: www.fas.org

As a nonpartisan, public policy research organization, the Federation of American Scientists (FAS) conducts evidence-based policy analysis examining the intersection between public policy and security and applied science and technology. While the organization was founded in 1945 with the intent of addressing the challenges posed by the development of nuclear weapons, FAS's mission has expanded to include biosecurity, energy security, and terrorism analysis. FAS's website provides detailed information about these topics and others relating both generally and specifically to war.

Heritage Foundation
214 Massachusetts Avenue NE, Washington, DC   20002-4999
(202) 546-4400
e-mail: info@heritage.org
website: www.heritage.org

The Heritage Foundation is a public policy think tank that has worked since its founding in 1973 to promote policies embodying conservative principles such as free enterprise, limited government, individual freedom, traditional American values, and a strong national defense. In accordance with this last value, the foundation has maintained the position that American armed forces must be poised to take action anywhere in the world to defend the country's safety and freedom. One important facet of this position is the maintenance of a powerful military that can help to enforce American policy and protect American interests. Under the umbrella of foreign and defense policy, Heritage Foundation scholars address war in connection with arms control and nonproliferation, international conflicts, and missile defense. Articles on these topics can be accessed on the foundation's website.

Human Rights Watch (HRW)

350 Fifth Avenue, 34th Floor, New York, NY   10118-3299
(212) 290-4700 • fax: (212) 736-1300
website: www.hrw.org

Human Rights Watch (HRW) is an organization that works on the international level to ensure and protect human rights for all people worldwide. Within its broad work on human rights, the impact of war as it relates to arms, cluster munitions, incendiary weapons, land mines, child soldiers, and war crimes has been explored extensively. HRW seeks to ensure that those who commit human rights abuses both within and outside of the war setting are held accountable for their actions. Articles on specific abuses that are taking place around the world as a result of war can be read on HRW's website.

Peace Action

Montgomery Center, 8630 Fenton Street, Suite 524
Silver Spring, MD   20910
(301) 565-4050 • fax: (301) 565-0850
e-mail: info@peace-action.org
website: www.peace-action.org

Peace Action is a national grassroots peace network that seeks to influence the US Congress and administration through a concerted effort of its national chapters and affiliates. By writing to the government, engaging in Internet and direct actions, and lobbying citizens, the organization attempts to promote peace legislation within the US government. The group's current antiwar issues include ending the wars in Afghanistan and Iraq, moving money from war to US communities, and preventing war in Iran. Details about the background of these initiatives and current actions being taken can be found on Peace Action's website.

United for Peace & Justice
Times Square Station, PO Box 607, New York, NY 10108
(212) 868-5545
website: www.unitedforpeace.org

United for Peace & Justice was founded in 2002 when more than seventy organizations dedicated to promoting peace and justice joined to create a new coalition with the goal of ending the war in Iraq. In the subsequent decade, the organization's work has expanded to include additional topics such as the war in Afghanistan, nuclear disarmament, war funding, and military spending. Details about these campaigns can be found on the organization's website.

US Department of Defense (US DOD)
1400 Defense Pentagon, Washington, DC 20301-1400
(703) 571-3343
website: www.defense.gov

The Department of Defense (DOD) is the US government department charged with maintaining the military forces necessary to prevent war and protect the country. Some of the top issues of concern for the DOD include the war in Afghanistan, warrior care, and cybersecurity. The DOD website provides information about the actions being taken within these and other areas to ensure the security of the United States.

World Policy Institute (WPI)
108 West Thirty-Ninth Street, Suite 1000
New York, NY 10018
(212) 481-5005 • fax: (212) 481-5009
e-mail: wpi@worldpolicy.org
website: www.worldpolicy.org

For fifty years, the World Policy Institute has strived to be a source of trusted nonpartisan, international policy information and leadership. The institute has sought to achieve a three-pronged goal: maintain an open and stable global market economy, promote knowledgeable civic participation at a global level to establish working governments, and foster international cooperation on security issues that impact both the nation and the world. War and conflict often surface as significant issues to be addressed within this framework, and articles under this umbrella, including "Meaningful Peace," "The Dangers of Launching a War Against Iran," and many others about conflicts in the Middle East, Africa, and Asia, can be read online.

Bibliography of Books

John Arquilla — *Insurgents, Raiders, and Bandits: How Masters of Irregular Warfare Have Shaped Our World.* Chicago, IL: Ivan R. Dee, 2011.

Abdel-Bari Atwan — *The Secret History of al-Qa'ida.* London: Saqi Books, 2006.

Peter L. Bergen — *The Longest War: The Enduring Conflict Between America and al-Qaeda.* New York: Free Press, 2011.

Nathan E. Busch and Daniel H. Joyner, eds. — *Combating Weapons of Mass Destruction: The Future of International Nonproliferation Policy.* Athens: University of Georgia Press, 2009.

Joseph Cirincione, Jon B. Wolfsthal, and Miriam Rajkumar — *Deadly Arsenals: Nuclear, Biological, and Chemical Threats.* Washington, DC: Carnegie Endowment for International Peace, 2005.

Dale C. Copeland — *The Origins of Major War.* Ithaca, NY: Cornell University Press, 2000.

Audrey Kurth Cronin — *How Terrorism Ends: Understanding the Decline and Demise of Terrorist Campaigns.* Princeton, NJ: Princeton University Press, 2009.

Mark Danner — *Torture and Truth: America, Abu Ghraib, and the War on Terror.* New York: New York Review of Books, 2004.

Ivan Eland — *No War for Oil: U.S. Dependency and the Middle East*. Oakland, CA: Independent Institute, 2011.

Richard N. Haass — *Intervention: The Use of American Military Force in the Post–Cold War World*. Washington, DC: Brookings Institution Press, 1999.

Chris Hedges — *War Is a Force That Gives Us Meaning*. New York: PublicAffairs, 2002.

Bruce Hoffman — *Inside Terrorism*. New York: Columbia University Press, 2006.

Seth G. Jones — *In the Graveyard of Empires: America's War in Afghanistan*. New York: Norton, 2010.

Mary Kaldor, Terry Lynn Karl, and Yahia Said, eds. — *Oil Wars*. London: Pluto, 2007.

Robert G. Kaufman — *In Defense of the Bush Doctrine*. Lexington: University Press of Kentucky, 2008.

David Kilcullen — *The Accidental Guerrilla: Fighting Small Wars in the Midst of a Big One*. New York: Oxford University Press, 2009.

Melvyn P. Leffler and Jeffrey W. Legro, eds. — *To Lead the World: American Strategy After the Bush Doctrine*. New York: Oxford University Press, 2008.

| Mark Malloch-Brown | *The Unfinished Global Revolution: The Pursuit of a New International Politics.* New York: Penguin, 2011. |

Alfred W. McCoy — *Torture and Impunity: The U.S. Doctrine of Coercive Interrogation.* Madison: University of Wisconsin Press, 2012.

Ahmed Rashid — *Taliban: Militant Islam, Oil and Fundamentalism in Central Asia.* New Haven, CT: Yale University Press, 2010.

Kenneth Roth and Minky Worden, eds. — *Torture: Does It Make Us Safer? Is It Ever OK?: A Human Rights Perspective.* New York: New Press, 2005.

Scott D. Sagan and Kenneth N. Waltz — *The Spread of Nuclear Weapons: An Enduring Debate.* 3rd edition. New York: Norton, 2012.

David E. Sanger — *Confront and Conceal: Obama's Secret Wars and Surprising Use of American Power.* New York: Crown, 2012.

Jessica Stern — *Terror in the Name of God: Why Religious Militants Kill.* New York: Ecco, 2003.

Michael Walzer — *Just and Unjust Wars: A Moral Argument with Historical Illustrations.* 4th edition. New York: Basic, 2006.

Bob Woodward — *Bush at War.* New York: Simon & Schuster, 2002.

Bob Woodward   *Obama's Wars*. New York: Simon & Schuster, 2010.

Howard Zinn   *Just War*. New York: Charta, 2006.

Index

J

K

L